Arthur Beckwith

**Majolica and fayence : Italian, Sicilian, Majorcan,
Hispano-Moresque and Persian**

Arthur Beckwith

Majolica and fayence : Italian, Sicilian, Majorcan, Hispano-Moresque and Persian

ISBN/EAN: 9783337229047

Printed in Europe, USA, Canada, Australia, Japan

Cover: Foto ©Andreas Hilbeck / pixelio.de

More available books at **www.hansebooks.com**

MAJOLICA

AND

FAYENCE:

ITALIAN, SICILIAN, MAJORCAN, HISPANO-MORESQUE, AND PERSIAN.

BY
ARTHUR BECKWITH.

WITH PHOTO-ENGRAVED ILLUSTRATIONS.

NEW YORK:
D. APPLETON AND COMPANY,
549 & 551 BROADWAY.
1877.

PREFACE.

THE interest shown by visitors in the ceramic display at the International Exhibition of 1876, and the indications of a growing appreciation of this phase of Art, led me to undertake to give some account of the development of Majolica and Fayence, the localities and distinguishing characteristics of its various manufactures, the subjects represented on many pieces, and a description of examples chosen for illustration, chiefly from the collection of Signor Castellani.

In the following pages, the purchaser of mediæval and modern Fayence will find notes that may be useful; while I have added, for those interested in painting on pottery in vitrifiable colors, an outline of this process, and also suggestions intended to assist the designer.

ARTHUR BECKWITH,
S. E. corner Church and Cortlandt Streets, New York.

January 3, 1877.

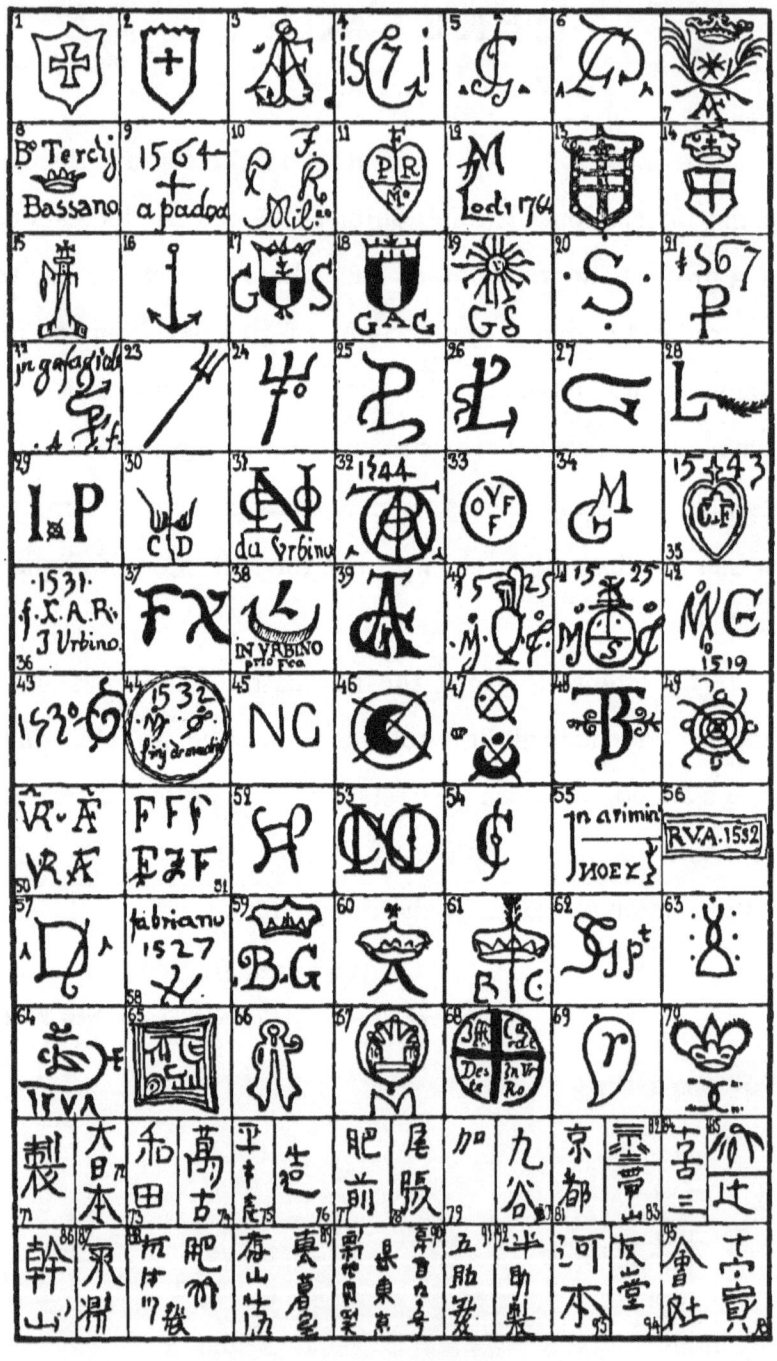

MARKS.

ITALIAN.—1. VENICE, about 1540, fabrique of Mo. Ludovico. 2. VENICE, about 1560. 3. VENICE, composed of A A F and triple anchor, said to be of 1650-1700, by Graesse ; Jacquemart gives a similar mark formed of A A R. 4. VENICE, 1571. 5. VENICE. 6. VENICE. 7. VENICE, 1753-'63, believed to be that of the brothers Bertolini, at Murano. 8. BASSANO, mark of Bo. Terchi. The five-pointed crown is found also at Castelli and at Naples ; at Naples it is closed on top. 9. PADUA, 1564 ; this cross is also seen on Paduan pieces, with the dates 1548, 1550, 1555, 1563. 10. MILAN, eighteenth century ; probably F. di Pasquale Rubati. 11. MILAN, eighteenth century, F. di Pasquale Rubati. 12. LODI, 1764. 13. TURIN, end of seventeenth century, shield of Savoy and crown. 14. TURIN, eighteenth century. 15. GENOA, lighthouse and beacon. 16. SAVONA. 17. SAVONA, sixteenth century, shield with initials, standing for Guidobono Savona, or Girolamo Salomone. 18. SAVONA, sixteenth century, mark of Gian. Antonio Guidobono ; the shield is also seen with the letters B C G. 19. SAVONA, Girolamo Salomone. 20. CAFFAGIOLO. 21. CAFFAGIOLO, 1567, on a jug numbered 39a in Signor Castellani's collection. 22. CAFFAGIOLO, about 1547. 23. CAFFAGIOLO, written over a trident. 24. CAFFAGIOLO, also attributed to Faenza, when placed in a crossed circle. 25. CAFFAGIOLO, surrounded by eight stars. 26. CAFFAGIOLO, first period of ornamental work. 27. CAFFAGIOLO. 28. MONTE LUPO, L and wolf's brush. 29. PESARO, in Pesaro. 30. CASTEL DURANTE, sketched from No. 179 of Signor Castellani's collection. 31. URBINO, Nicola da Urbino monogram. 32. ORAZIO FONTANA, 1544. 33. URBINO, O F V F (Orazio Fontana Urbino fecit), according to Passeri. 34. URBINO, Giamaria Mariani, of Urbino. 35. URBINO, Guido Fontana, 1543. 36. URBINO, 1531, Francesco Xanto Avelli da Rovigo in Urbino, early signature. 37. URBINO, Francesco Xanto, his later signature when better known. 38. URBINO. 39. GUBBIO, monogram of Maestro Georgio Andreoli. 40. GUBBIO, signature of Mo. Georgio Andreoli. 41. The same. 42. Probably the same, 1519. 43. The same, 1530. 44. The same, 1532, with *fini di maiolica* (" the finest of majolica "). Other signatures are given in the illustrations of Gubbio pieces at the left hand of the figures ; they are in lustre pigment. 45. NOCERA. 46. FAENZA, Casa Pirota fabrique. 47. FAENZA, Casa Pirota. 48. FAENZA of 1520. 49. FAENZA, Casa Pirota. 50. FAENZA. 51. FAENZA, variously-formed F. 52. FORLI. 53. FAENZA, the monogram of Nicolo da Fano, who probably worked at Faenza. 54. DERUTA. 55. RIMINI, two forms of Rimini mark. 56. RAVENNA, 1532. 57. DERUTA, about 1539. 58. FABRIANO, 1527. 59. NAPLES, Franco Brandi. 60. NAPLES. 61. NAPLES, five-pointed crown, closed, and feathered. 62. CASTELLI, Saverio Grue pinxit.

PERSIAN.—63. PERSIAN, unknown factory. 64. PERSIAN, Muhamed Ali, 1278 of the Hegira, or 1861 A. D. 65. PERSIAN, on a flask in the possession of Mr. Fortnum.

HISPANO-MORESQUE.—66. HISPANO-MORESQUE, about 1480. 67. HISPANO-MORESQUE, dated 1610. 68. HISPANO-MORESQUE, probably made at Manises in 1613, for the Illustrissimo Signore Cardinale d'Este in Urbe Romæ. 69. HISPANO-MORESQUE. 70. MADRID.

JAPANESE.—71. TSAE signifies "made." 72. TAI-NI-PON, Great Japan (read from top to bottom). 73. AWATA, often seen on Awata ware. 74. BANKO. 75. HIRA-DO-SON, egg-shell porcelain. 76. TZOU signifies "maker." 77. HITZEN, porcelain. 78. OWARI, porcelain. 79. KAGA. 80. KUTANI, "nine valleys," often on Kaga ware. 81. KIYOTO. 82. ITSIGAYA, in seal character, a place in Satsuma, marked on Satsuma ware. 83. TAIZAN, maker's name. 84. Kisa, the mark of S. Fukaomi. 85. KORANSHA, trade-mark ; below it is the mark of K. Tsuji. 86. Kanzan Denshichi. 87. Zengara Yeiraku. 88. Y. Fukagawa. 89. M. Kozan. 90. Hiyochiyen. 91. Gosuke. 92. Hansuke. 93. Kawamoto. 94. K. Shinoda. 95. Shippo Kuwaisha, read from top to bottom, beginning with the right-hand column.

Authorities.—The marks 1, 3, 5, 7, 9, 12, 17, 22, 31, 32, 39, 40, 43, 44, 44, 46, 49, 57, 58, 64, 65, are copied from Fortnum.

Nos. 2, 4, 10, 11, 13, 14, 15, 18, 19, 24, 35, 38, 45, 48, 51, 55, 56, 62, 63, 66, 67, 69, 70, are from Dr. Th. Graesse.

Nos. 6, 8, 16, 23, 26, 27, 28, 29, 33, 34, 36, 37, 41, 42, 47, 50, 52, 53, 54, 59, 60, 61, are from Jacquemart.

Nos. 21 and 25 are from Signor Castellani's collection.

Nos. 73, 74, 75, 77, 78, 79, 81, 82, 83, are from W. H. Hooper.

Nos. 30, 71, 72, 76, 80, 84, 85, 86, 87, 88, 89, 90, 91, 92, 93, 94, 95, were sketched by the writer from various pieces in the Exhibition of 1876.

The above are some of the principal marks of fayence. In the hand-books of Messrs. Chaffers, Graesse, Hooper, and others, are some two or three thousand marks relating to pottery generally.

ILLUSTRATIONS.

THE illustrations in these pages, figured Nos. 1 to 39, and 46 to 49, inclusive, represent pieces of pottery exhibited in the collection of Signor Alessandro Castellani, of Rome, at the International Exhibition of 1876.

I take pleasure in acknowledging the liberal spirit in which Signor Castellani permitted me to sketch, without restriction, the objects in his beautiful collection, to many of which an artistic and historical interest is attached. The other sketches are from various other collections.

These pen-and-ink sketches are reproduced by the process of photo-engraving, which, by mechanical means, makes metal blocks, in which the lines of the original drawing are obtained in relief, and which can be printed from with little more care than is required for ordinary type. Enlargement or reduction of size is also readily obtained; in this instance the reduction is forty per cent. in the linear dimensions. This convenient and labor-saving process has not yet received the development of which it is susceptible. Messrs. Leggo Brothers, 39 Park Row, New York, photo-engraved the blocks, and Mr. David Carr, 98 Nassau Street, New York, electrotyped them.

CONTENTS.

	PAGE
PREFACE	3
MARKS	4
ILLUSTRATIONS	6
USE OF MAJOLICA	9

DEVELOPMENT IN ITALY:

Movement of Art in Italy	13
Introduction of Various Processes in Italy	21
Development of Majolica in Italy under Successive Governments	24
Della Robbia Ware	27
Technical Notes on Majolica and Fayence	30
Inscriptions on Italian Majolica and Fayence	32
Venetian States: *Venice, Treviso, Bassano, Nove, Padua, Candiana, Verona*	37
Lombardy: *Milan, Lodi*	40
Sardinia: *Turin, Laforest*	41
States of Genoa: *Genoa, Savona, Arbisola*	42
Northern Duchies: *Ferrara, Modena, Reggio, Sassuolo, Mantua*	42
Tuscany: *Caffagiolo, Siena, Pisa, Florence, Asciano, Monte Lupo, San Quirigo, Borgo*	44
Duchies of Urbino: *Pesaro, Castel Durante, Urbino, Gubbio, Nocera, Castello, Bagnolo*	54
The Marches: *Faenza, Forli, Rimini, Imola, Ravenna, Bologna*	92

CONTENTS.

	PAGE
States of the Church: *Deruta, Fabriano, Foligno, Spello, Viterbo, Rome*	99
Southern Italy: *Naples, Grotaglia, Castelli, Palermo, Catala Girone*	102
Graffiti	105

PERSIA:

Persian Fayence: *History, Ornament, Symbolism, Technical Notes, Modern Copies*	106
Rhodian Fayence: *History, Characteristics*	123
Anatolian, Damascus, Roumanian	124
Sicilian, Siculo-Persian, Siculo-Moresque: *History, Characteristics*	126
Majorcan: *History, Characteristics*	135
Hispano-Moresque: *Malaga, Valencia, Barcelona*, Nic. Francisco	136

ART	143
PROPOSITIONS IN ORNAMENT	152
HINTS FOR PAINTING ON POTTERY	158
MISCELLANEOUS NOTES, SYMBOLS, ITALIAN DESIGNATIONS, PRICES IN THE SIXTEENTH CENTURY	163
MODERN FAYENCE AT THE EXHIBITION OF 1876	167
REFERENCES	184

USE OF MAJOLICA.

The Abbé Passeri, a lover of art, deplored the taste that in 1758 preferred Oriental porcelains, with ornaments which he said were no better than those seen on playing-cards, to the Italian majolica, embellished with designs full of thought and feeling; and he added with some bitterness, "The inferior part of man will be in favor of Eastern porcelain, but the rational and intellectual will guide him to majolica."

Whatever there may be of truth, if any, in the abbé's remark, will become apparent, I trust, in the following pages.

Public taste of the present day, it will doubtless be admitted, demands in every branch of art brilliant technical effects and great accuracy in minute details, but shows less regard for high conceptions, and both artists and artisans are obliged to yield in a measure to this demand. The last half-century has witnessed sudden and rapid progress in material science, the mechanical handling of matter, the manipulation of metals, the composition of enamels and dyes, the weaving of textiles; and attention seems at last limited almost entirely to the domain of material facts. The study of science trains the mind to accuracy of observation of details, rather than of the beauties of Nature, and art is tested, as it were, by the rules of geometry. An unsymmetrical leaf, a figure repeated with a change, a ground-color that varies or pulsates, a line shaken by the vibrations of the hand, have come to be considered fatal errors in ornament. Inferior composition, absence of action, or a meagre, realistic style, is readily overlooked or pardoned in works that display the so-called "conscientious accuracy" in details of minor importance; but woe to the artist who is not also a geographer and an archæologist, a chemist and geologist, for his critic is likely to be all of these!

The spread among us, through the widening channels of commerce, of rich and gorgeous products of the East, makes us by contrast sensible of the frequent poverty of native decoration and ornament. The publication and diffusion of designs and pictures of Eastern life tend to the same result. Leading writers on ornament acknowledge the beauty of Oriental decoration, and this has encouraged in some instances the formation of a school of copyists.

The substitution of perfected models in place of crude forms is easy and natural; but the custom of mere copying tends to stifle the growth of the originality which is frequently the best feature, and should characterize the products of every nation. Still more detrimental is the copying of inferior designs for the sake of novelty, as may be seen to-day in Japan, in some instances where native manufacturers reproduce poorer sorts of European designs. But there is a way to avoid these errors, and procure all the benefit to be derived from perfected models: it consists in studying the principles and methods applied in the production of these combinations, and in applying these principles in works characteristic of our national tastes, manners, customs, habits, and scenes.

It is possible to adopt with advantage certain parts of foreign ornament, but this requires discrimination. Fitness and good taste demand careful selection and rejection.

The errors of treatment in Sèvres and Berlin porcelain have been reproduced by copyists. Unlike the Renaissance artists, these manufactories too frequently adopted, for painting in enamel colors, a treatment only suitable to painting in oil on canvas. The attempt to cover the whole surface of a piece of pottery with elaborate colors is not easily made successful, as the effect is often more agreeable when certain clear spaces of fine, pure enamel are left untouched.

Again, convex surfaces are often treated as if they were flat. Elaborate landscapes appear with human figures in the foreground, on rolling surfaces, presenting no point of view from which the figures are not denaturalized and painfully distorted. Errors of this kind result in misapplied art, and may easily be avoided. Oriental taste selects ornaments for uneven surfaces which adapt themselves to the forms, and seem rarely out of place.

Beautiful as are many specimens of European and Oriental porcelain, the Italian majolica of the sixteenth century frequently surpasses them in lively harmonious effect.

In this connection I may briefly allude to a different order of decoration—that of interiors, dining-rooms, libraries, and other apartments, in which the decorated pieces of pottery are in turn used as elements of ornament. For this purpose majolica holds the first rank. Lustred pieces of this ware, selected with taste and arranged with skill on a suitable background, against walls or upon shelves, produce charming effects. Unlustred Italian fayence, often inferior in brilliancy of enamel to Oriental porcelain, frequently surpasses it in softness and harmony of tones, and contrasts more agreeably with the surroundings, while the subjects are usually more pleasing and more readily appreciated. Decorations of this double character, combining considerable thought, study, and imagination, with skill, taste, and feeling, afford pleasing and unfailing subjects of contemplation, and appeal effectively to the higher feelings and æsthetic tastes of every grade of cultivation and refinement.

Modern pottery has not, in some respects, attained this degree of excellence, but its prospects and its promise are gratifying. Materials of the best quality, enamel colors, and facilities for firing them, abound; the disposition and skill required to develop their use are manifest, and the great schools of Nature and the past are open to all. The elements on one side are abundant, while their complement, to be found in the public taste and demand, is pronounced in all directions with increased emphasis.

If Italians of the sixteenth century could afford to have superb pottery of excellent designs, manufactured for their family use and for presents, rather than for sale, and to which we are indebted for much that is beautiful in this department, there seems no good reason why any household of the nineteenth century should be destitute of similar pieces, displaying the taste and cultivation of the family circle, and diffusing at all times a pleasing and refining influence.

DEVELOPMENT IN ITALY.

MOVEMENT OF ART IN ITALY.

IN art, as in Nature, each phase appears to grow with variations out of preceding phases. The origin of great social, industrial, or artistic movements must be sought in periods long antecedent to their apparent birth and power.

Any attempt to trace fully the origin of the art which characterized the great Art-epochs in Italy would extend beyond the range of these pages. But the streams of thought which flowed from Egypt and Assyria and united in the Levant are curiously illustrated in the Cesnola Cyprian collection (Metropolitan Museum, New York). Those familiar with the Egyptian and Assyrian will readily recognize the blending of the types.

Egypto-Assyrian influence in art found an early channel of diffusion in the enterprise of the Phœnicians, whose commercial voyages and trading-stations embraced the waters of the Mediterranean, and extended along the Atlantic shores to Britain and Ireland. The Egypto-Assyrian influence is nowhere more distinctly shown than in the statuary of the Etruscans, in their beautiful pottery, and in the instructive collection from Præneste. That the Romans took their first notions of art from the Etruscans is manifest from the numerous rude copies of Etruscan mortuary sculpture disclosed by the excavations along the Appian Way.

But the Romans were never strong in art, with the exception of the department of architecture. In this they were bold and grand, and they imparted to it an originality and vigor highly characteristic of the race that conquered and ruled the Western world for a thousand years. But in sculpture and painting, and in the decorative and industrial arts, they displayed no qualities of note until they came in contact with the matured art of Greece. Greek art may be said to have been transferred bodily to Rome, by the transfer of Greek artists, who continued to reproduce there their native art. Many of these artists were prisoners of war and slaves, to whom the Romans owed their best art, as they did one of their earliest reliable historians, the Greek scholar Polybius, a prisoner of war and a slave. To this source also is the world indebted for much of the so-called "antique" forming the great collections of Rome.

Greek art became popular and abundant in Rome; but it never rose in the hands of the Romans to anything more notable than inferior copies made upon Greek models. The Romans were thoroughly material and practical. They never displayed the æsthetic skill and taste of the Greeks. When Constantine, 330 A. D., transferred the seat of empire to Constantinople, Greco-Roman art had declined, but many of its rich monuments remained, until the successive invasions of the Goths destroyed large portions; and, later still, the Christian emperors, in their hatred of what they considered the remains of paganism, nearly completed the destruction.

A reaction, however, set in: fathers of the Church discovered, almost too late, and proved, that *the Bible favors art*, and St. Basilius declared that *art disposes to virtue*. The Christians in turn erected, from the ruins they had wrought, basilicas in a style now called *Latin;* this style was a rude copy of the Roman: in decoration the nude was covered with drapery, and a touch of austerity and asceticism prevailed, as seen in the sarcophagi of the fourth and fifth centuries and the paintings in the catacombs.

In the fifth century a change appears, and the *Byzantine*, also called *Neo-Grec*, is introduced, with its walls decorated with mosaic, painting, and sculpture; the change of ornamental forms may be studied in the ivory diptychs of the fourth to the ninth century. In the north, the Lombards, who had conquered and ruled in Lombardy from the sixth to the eighth century, introduced a heavy, austere, debased Roman style, called the *First Lombard style*.

In the eleventh century, the commerce between Genoa, Venice, and the East, had taken a large development, and the crusades commenced; the Latin is in turn transformed by a larger infusion of the Byzantine, and gives birth to the *Romanesque, Lombard of the second period*, or *Italian*. In 1066 the Abbé Désiré brought mosaic artisans from Constantinople, and a Byzantine school of painting was established in Rome. Theophanes opened a similar school at Venice, and in about 1230 Sienna and Pisa followed in the same path. This second Lombard style lasted from the eleventh to the thirteenth century.

In Sicily, where the Arabs had erected fine monuments in the tenth century, a peculiar style arose, which reached its maturity in the twelfth century. It was a mixture of the Byzantine, Arabic, and second Lombard. This Arab element also crept into Italy, and Venice showed, in its twelfth-century arch, the Arab or Persian influence.

Meantime *Gothic* architecture had obtained considerable expansion in Northern Europe, and found its way into Italy. It is characterized by the prevalence of vertical lines, more than by the pointed arch or probably any other feature. The "pointed arch" was used by the Assyrians in the eighth century B. C. It is seen in Persian architecture in the Mosque of Tabreez and Tower of Yezd. The Arabs adopted it in Cairo in the seventh century A. D.; it is seen there in the Ebn-Touloun Mosque built A. D. 885, and in Sicily in Arab monuments of the tenth century. It appears in Germany subsequent to the Norman invasion of Sicily, 1060 A. D.; but it is gradually modified to suit the exigencies of the vertical element, and becomes more pointed. The severity of the earlier Gothic admitted of but little ornament, but this severity was gradually relaxed, and the *Florid Gothic* appeared, with profuse ornaments borrowed from many sources, including a large portion of Byzantine and Persian in the best examples, but not without numerous deplorable departures from what in principle distinguishes the Gothic.

We now approach the period known as the *Renaissance*, an era of revival of letters, science, and art, characterized by the shaking off of trammels imposed by existing methods. Art especially took new life, and owed its vitality to a return to the direct study of Nature and of classic antiquity, and the absence of servile copying. This movement began in the thirteenth century, and attained great development in the fifteenth and sixteenth centuries. The Medici princes encouraged researches in literature and art. Their court became the active centre of men of science and artists. Prominent citizens followed their example, and art and science became a path to social distinction. Men of ability and originality, of genius and invention, who at other times would have been philosophers and statesmen, turned their attention to art, and gave it an importance and development it had never before reached in Western Europe. Their influence is felt even at this day in every department.

The plan of this sketch does not admit of more than a brief mention of a few conspicuous men who mark the progress of the movement, and were mostly founders of styles, around which clustered the various schools. In proportion as a work approaches perfection, every blemish or omission is rendered more conspicuous by contrast. Hence nothing is easier, in general, than to point out faults in the best of human productions. On the other hand, few things are more rare than a just and complete appreciation of merits and defects, without which critical judgment is imperfect and unsound. In this connection the progress of the Renaissance forms a subject of most profitable study.

Niccola Pisano (1206–1278), architect, sculptor, and painter, a man of versatile and vigorous genius, impressed by the beauty

NATURE AND CLASSIC ANTIQUITY. 17

of the remains of Greek sculpture, threw off the constrained manner of his contemporaries and became the founder of a school of SCULPTURE based on the imitation of Nature in the manner practised by the Greeks. The excellence of the results of this principle was soon appreciated, and numerous men of note followed in this path. Thus, *Andrea Pisano* (1270-1345), who sculptured the great gate of bronze of the Baptistery of San Giovanni at Florence; *Giovanni Pisano* (1240-1320); *Orcagna* (1328-1389), whose style is seen in the Baldachino of Or San Michele, Florence; *Ghiberti* (1378-1455), celebrated for his somewhat realistic bronze gates of the same baptistery as Andrea's; and *Donatello* (1383-1466), successfully adopted the principle of Niccola of Pisa. *Luca della Robbia* (1400-1481) at this time introduced modeling in enameled terra-cotta, and his style was pure and simple; and finally appears in sculpture the vigorous hand of *Michael Angelo* (1474-1564), who possessed the skill and resolution required to arrest his works at the stage of greatest suggestiveness, leaving them in that condition of lively promise so rarely, if ever, realized by completion.

In ARCHITECTURE Florence took the lead in the revival. *Brunelleschi* (1377-1446) built the Pitti Palace, and the Tuscan school followed his teachings. Fortunate researches brought to light the books of Vitruvius, a Roman architect of the first century B. C. *Alberti* (1404-1484) published a celebrated work; *Bramante* (1444-1514) led in the Roman school, and designed the Tortonia Palace and St. Peter's, which was continued by Raphael and Peruzzi, and nearly completed by Michael Angelo. *Baldassare Peruzzi* (1481-1536) built the Farnesina Palace; *Raphael* (1483-1520) designed the Pandolfini Palace at Florence; *Michael Angelo* (1474-1564) designed the dome of St. Peter's, the Porta Pia, and the present Capitol; *Vignola* (1507-1573) altered St. Peter's somewhat, and published a well-known work; *Palladio's* work (1518-1580) also appeared; and *Bernini* (1598-1680) completed St. Peter's by additions of a picturesque and quaint or *baroque* nature.

In Milan, *Leonardo da Vinci* (1452-1519) was known as an

architect and engineer, as well as a painter and sculptor; and in Venice *Jacopo Sansovino* (1479-1570) built the Library of St. Mark.

In Renaissance architecture the features adopted were chiefly Greek and Roman, and in decoration Greek, Roman, and Arab.

In PAINTING, *Cimabue* (1240-1301) opened the new era. He abandoned the meagre Byzantine school in vogue, returned to the study of Nature, gave free play to his original and inventive genius, and with his strong coloring produced vigorous effects.

Giotto, a shepherd (1276-1337), educated by Cimabue, followed him in adhering to Nature, but surpassed him in grace. His colors were harmonious, his lines flowing, and his design partook of the elegance of antique statuary. The principles thus introduced developed new results at the disposal of the painter.

Paolo Ucello (1389-1472), *Pier della Francesca* (1398-1484), and *Brunelleschi* (1377-1446), perfected the study of perspective.

Masaccio (1401-1443) made an advance in the fine relief and life-like spirit imparted to his work, but carried his leaning to Nature in a wrong direction by introducing portraits of his friends in historical pieces.

Ghirlandaio (1451-1495) obtained breadth of style by studying another art, and laid down the rule that "drawing is the whole picture, but mosaic is painting for eternity"—a most useful principle when rightly understood.

Signorelli (1440-1521) was one of the first to apply a thorough knowledge of anatomy to painting, but his style was dry.

Leonardo da Vinci (1452-1519), engineer, architect, sculptor, painter, and anatomist—observing, penetrating, analytical; remarkable for the scope and variety of his attainments. He studied aërial perspective, preferred a diffused light as the most becoming, inculcated unremitting observation of Nature, and rapid sketching of the human figure in actual movement under the influence of various emotions and passions; and his solicitude for the progress of art earned for him the name of "the Father of Painting." He excelled in technical execution and in refined expression of character. His "Christ," at Milan, is a wonder of art. The expression is lofty and calm; the countenance luminous and subdued—an inward, contemplative look that includes the past and future in the present as one; deep feeling, boundless compassion, a mournful yet cheerful aspect; with a tinge of absence that indicates ultimate thoughts reaching to the unseen.

Michael Angelo (1474-1564), a universal and rugged genius, showing less solicitude for elegance and beauty than for the expression of vigor; of great power, and with a fertility of imagination that obliterates historical facts. His work shows a captivating strength of will and amazing facility of expression.

Titian (1477-1576), unsurpassed in rich natural color, and in the contrast of color producing brilliant tints, his favorite light deep and glowing. He was superior to his time in landscape, as in the "Peter Martyr," and unrivaled in portraits.

Giorgione (1477-1511) introduced a free, bold, determined touch, that discarded minuteness; he was noted as a colorist, and for natural middle tints.

Raphael Sanzio (1483-1520) reflects throughout his career the spiritual strength of the Umbrian school. Although surpassed by others in many of the individual qualities of art, probably none combined so many in a superior degree. Infinite grace, an impassioned sense of the beautiful, fertility of conception, elegance of composition, charming color, admirable design, and breadth of treatment, are among his characteristics. His compositions are not free from anachronisms, but it is difficult to decide how much of this is due to his patrons, or to a desire to adopt a grandeur of style suited to all time. By the middle of the sixteenth century the Roman (Raphael's) school of painting had become predominant throughout Italy.

Andrea del Sarto (1488-1530) was eminent for correct outlines, good taste, and graceful expression of the feelings and passions.

Correggio (1494-1534), superb in flesh-color, remarkable for his knowledge of light and shade, and atmospheric effects; also for his preference for pleasing objects and joyous countenances. His drapery was admirable.

Tintoretto (1512-1594), greatly applauded by some. His works are remarkable for strong *chiaro-oscuro*, a dark scale of colors, and for vigorous action rather than grace; his motto was, " Michael Angelo's design and Titian's coloring."

Timoteo Viti (1500-1524), a pupil of Raphael, carried that school to Urbino; and painting on pottery was raised to a fine art by the works of *Giorgio* of Gubbio, *Brandani*, *Rovigo*, and especially *Orazio* and *Flaminio Fontana* (1540), who brought this art to its highest point, and worked with great success. Many industrial arts were influenced in the same way, and produced objects of great beauty.

In the seventeenth century political troubles appeared; dissensions among the republics had led to the rule of despotic and corrupt princes; displays of inconsistent vanity prevailed; taste in art became pompous and heavy, sensual and confused. The *Caracci* arrested for a while the descent, and the *Eclectic* school arose, with high aims but moderate talent. The followers of the great masters imitated more the superficial signs of their greatness than their excellent methods, and often fell into affectation and mannerism. On the other hand, a school of *naturalisti* arose, who neglected the æsthetic aim of art, and professed to study Nature only; but many of this school, by ignoring the beautiful, took only a one-sided view of Nature, and aimed at a dramatic display of the repulsive, frequently devoid of any moral end.

The spirit of the Renaissance almost vanished from the place of its origin, but took root and survived in other countries, where with various modifications it continues to flourish.

The nineteenth century, in Italy, presents another change equally striking and much more pleasing. Politically united and regenerated, the country shows signs of recovering its ancient distinction and renown, and its promises in this are uniformly welcomed and accepted with confidence.

INTRODUCTION OF VARIOUS PROCESSES IN ITALY.

From the time when the Etruscan potter Marcus wrote in Tyrrheno-Pelasgic characters, upon an unbaked crater found at Cære, "IUUNA—LAPHTI—MARKEI—KURIEAS—KLUTHI—IUKE," or, "Know you not the skilled potter Mark?" pottery of clay baked and unbaked has been known in Italy.

Pottery of baked clay coated with a soft lead-glaze and colored in yellow, green, and black, was known throughout the north of Europe and Italy before the eighth century, and was made by processes familiar to the Romans.

The custom prevailed in the eleventh, twelfth, and thirteenth centuries, of inlaying the outer surfaces of walls of churches and church-towers, and occasionally private residences, with slabs of porphyry, serpentine, and glazed earthenware. Some discussion has arisen as to the origin of the pieces of pottery the lustre of which attracts attention. Sismondi states that these plates are either Italian of the eleventh century or of Pesaro manufacture of the fourteenth century; while Marryat contends that the *bacini* or dishes are of Moorish pattern and origin, and attributes them to Majorca. Fortnum, on examination, thinks them with an exception Italian, but admits the possibility of an Oriental origin. He describes them as unlustred, lead-glazed ware, generally of white ground with arabesques of brownish yellow, birds, crosses, knots, stars, etc. But some have a blue ground; some are merely blue without other ornament; and others are covered with a slip of white clay, and decorated with *sgraffiato* ornaments. They are found incrusted in churches of Pesaro, Ancona, Pavia, Borgo Ticino, all of the eleventh and twelfth centuries; also in churches at Bologna and Rome. A Persian piece has been found imbedded in San Andrea at Pisa, and E. Piot mentions that he found Persian tiles incrusted in white marble in the church of San Giovanni del

Torro de Ravello, near Naples, in masonry of the thirteenth century.

The origin of the lustre with which Italian pottery is frequently enriched is attributed to various sources, but there is little doubt that it was derived from Persia direct, or through the Saracens.

The coating of pottery with rich iridescent lustres, first seen in Persia, is found successively on Arabic, Moorish, Hispano-Moresque, Siculo-Moresque, and Italian pottery. In all these cases the ornamental forms are Persian or derived from the Persian. Arabic and Moresque decoration, and the ornament of the early Italian lustred pieces of Pesaro, are also of Persian origin. These facts being admitted, the question whether or not the art of lustring in Italy was introduced by colonies of Moorish artisans who fled from persecution in Spain and established themselves in the Papal States, or whether it was brought direct from Persia by way of the Adriatic port of Pesaro, becomes of secondary consequence.

The first use of lustre in Italy is not traced to an earlier date than the latter half of the fifteenth century, and it was first applied upon lead-glazed wares, which were distinguished under the name of *mezza-majolica*, or half-majolica. The term *majolica* was then used only to designate the wares coming from the island of Majorca; subsequently, when the use of tin enamel upon terra-cotta became known in Italy, pieces coated with the stanniferous enamel, and lustred, were also called *majolica*. Of the origin of this name there can be no doubt. *Maiolica* is the name given by early Tuscan writers to the island of Majorca; Dante speaks also of the island of "Cipri e Maiolica." That this term was applied at first in Italy to the lustred ware, is shown by a dish beautifully painted and lustred, inscribed upon the back "*fini di Maiolica*," or *the finest of majolica*, and signed by Maestro Giorgio.

It was not until the middle of the sixteenth century that the term majolica was applied in Italy to many varieties of glazed earthenware; other countries followed this departure, and to-day a large class of wares is frequently called majolica which should properly be termed fayence, for it bears no resemblance to the products of Majorca, and resembles technically the unlustred glazed and enameled terra-cotta of Faenza.

In these pages both for convenience and accuracy the use of *the word majolica will be restricted to its original meaning* of lustred stanniferous glazed pottery.

The earliest date found on an Italian lustred piece is of the year 1489. The manufacturers of Pesaro, Gubbio, and Diruta, were the chief if not the only ones acquainted with the use of lustre, and after a career of some eighty years it fell suddenly into disuse and became a lost art about 1570.

Maestro Giorgio's lustred pieces are dated from 1518 to 1541, although he was still living in 1552. Francesco Xanto's work is dated 1530 to 1542.

In modern days the practice has been to a certain extent revived with varying success, but the new lustres are inferior in beauty to the old models.

Majolica will be treated in detail further on, but we will mention here some characteristics of the earlier mezza-majolica ware : The body is usually of a buff clay, and coated with a lustrous lead-glaze, or coated first with a slip of white clay, from San Giovanni, before being glazed. The outlines of the decoration are traced in manganese-black, or in blue, and the flesh is left of the color of the white slip, or shaded in blue. The lustres of *madreperla*, and *golden lustre*, which was simply a yellow color overlaid with the madreperla, are unsurpassed. The ornament is Moresque, and portraits of princes of the Sforza family are found. Toward the end of the fifteenth century lustred pieces with ornaments in relief were made.

The introduction of a stanniferous enamel in Italy occurred previous to its use by Luca della Robbia, who rather improved upon its quality than invented it; his first important piece bears the date of 1438. Other Italian pieces bear the dates 1475, 1477, 1482, 1486, 1487, 1489, 1491.

Previous to that we find it used in Spain and Majorca, and

in ancient times upon Babylonian tiles; while in Germany it was used at Schlettstadt in 1207, and took some development in that country in the thirteenth, fourteenth, and fifteenth centuries.

After Della Robbia, who died in 1481, various Italian manufactories adopted the tin enamel for general use, and it has continued in favor up to this time, together with the slips of white clay and the ordinary lead-glazes.

It may be questioned whether the praise frequently bestowed upon the stanniferous enamel as a basis of decoration is well founded; a ware with a white or slightly-tinted body, or coated with a slip of white clay, is better for color, as the tin of the enamel has a marked tendency to absorb and alter, or destroy, many colors laid upon it.

It is remarkable that the discernment which adopted the Persian processes of lustres and opaque stanniferous enamels should not have adopted at the same time (excepting in Sicily) the valuable Persian process of coating with a *silicious* glaze of great hardness, brilliancy, and durability.

DEVELOPMENT OF MAJOLICA IN ITALY UNDER SUCCESSIVE GOVERNMENTS.

The revival and development of pottery in Italy after the Gothic invasions must be attributed to the influence of the flourishing commerce of the ports of Venice, Pesaro, Genoa, and the inland city of Pisa, with the East, and to the liberal spirit of the Medici of Florence.

That the production of the earlier and coarser ware known as *mezza-majolica* was carried on at *Pesaro*, appears from the researches of Passeri, who finds the coats of arms of families of Pesaro, among others the Bergnana family, upon early plates with madreperla lustre, and the Pesaro archives mention one Pedrinus Joannis as being a *boccalari* there in 1396. Under *Costanza Sforza*, pieces with ornaments in relief, and better glazed, appear. In 1478 he sent to Sixtus IV. certain *vasa fic-*

tilia. His illegitimate son, *Giovanni Sforza*, of Aragon, Count of Pesaro, who succeeded him in 1483, and paid tribute to the Holy See, issued a decree in 1486, forbidding " both to citizens and foreigners (be their station what it may) to import any earthen vessels whatsoever, whether for ornament or otherwise, manufactured beyond the territory of Pesaro, with the exception of oil and water jars," and justifies this action by the desire to benefit the city of Pesaro, and by the priority of the art of vase-making in Pesaro, where it was " carried to greater perfection than in any other part of Italy, and is still extensively manufactured at Pesaro, attracting the admiration of all Italy and other countries." A fine dish in the collection of Mr. Fountaine, bearing two portraits, supposed to be those of young Sforza and his consort, Camilla da Marsano, and blank scroll overhead, is said, on slight grounds, to commemorate this edict.

The duchies of Ferrara, Rimini, and Ravenna, to some extent encouraged the art at this period, but the duchy of Urbino was the seat of the principal development of majolica in Italy.

The *first Duke of Urbino* was of the house of Montefeltro, and died in 1444. His illegitimate brother, *Federigo*, who succeeded him, married in 1460 Battista Sforza, built a castle at Urbino, decorated it highly, and generally encouraged the manufacture of majolica; under this prince Luca della Robbia worked. On the death of Federigo in 1482, his son, *Guidobaldo I.*, succeeded to him. In 1488 Guidobaldo married Elisabeta Gonzaga, of Mantua, engaged in war against Cæsar Borgia, lost in succession Pesaro and Faenza in 1502, and Urbino itself in 1503; he was restored in the same year to his plundered city, where he died in 1508. Under this prince the stanniferous enamel coating the whole piece began to be used, in about 1482 at Faenza, Florence, and Urbino, and in about 1500 at Pesaro, where some pieces of superior whiteness were misnamed *porcellana.*

The first *dated* lustred piece of 1489 is of his time, although the lustring was earlier practised at Pesaro under the Sforzas.

Giorgio Andreoli, of Pavia, and his brothers Salimbene and

Giovanni, came to Gubbio about 1485, where they were well received, and enrolled as citizens in 1498, on pain of forfeiting five hundred ducats if they left the city and the practice of the ceramic art. Giorgio adopted at that time the title of *maestro*, and later he was made *Castellano* of Gubbio; his signed lustred pieces date of the following reign.

In 1508 Guidobaldo I. was succeeded by his nephew, *Francesco Maria della Rovere*. Pope Leo X. forced him to retire from his duchy, but he was reinstated in 1517. He married Leonora Gonzago, daughter of Francesco, Marquis of Mantua, built the richly-decorated Imperial Palace at Pesaro, and patronized particularly the manufacture of Gubbio, employing Raffaele dal Colle or del Borgo to design for majolica; the lustred work of Mo. Giorgio attained its highest perfection during his reign; he died of poison at Pesaro in 1538.

Guidobaldo II. succeeded him from 1538 to 1574. Noted for extravagance, toward the end of his reign the state finances became involved, and there was a rapid decline in the patronage and the production of the duchy of Urbino. He made presents of services of majolica to the Emperor Charles V., to Philip II. of Spain, to his confessor, Frate Andrea de Volterra, and ordered for his medical dispensary a large set of vases, celebrated as the *Spezieria* vases, some of which are still to be seen. He allowed the art of lustring to fall into disuse, but took great pains to obtain perfect designs and outlines from the best models. For this object he collected drawings of Raphael and engravings of Marc Antonio, and procured original designs for majolica, to be made by the Venetian painter Battisto Franco, by Raffaele dal Colle, Orazio Fontana, and other painters of note. The decoration called *Raffaelesque*, and the pieces with designs after Raphael, called *Raffaele ware*, prevailed at this time, some twenty years or more after the death of Raffaele Sanzio of Urbino, who was born 1483 and died 1520. In other instances the decoration of majolica took, however, a mistaken direction, and we find a contemporary praising some pieces for their likeness to a painting in oil.

FIRST EUROPEAN PORCELAIN.

During the reign of Guidobaldo II. the productions of Pesaro attained their greatest perfection about 1540; and the fabriques of Castel Durante, one of which was directed by the Cavaliere Cipriano Piccolpasso, also excelled. Piccolpasso's work, "The Three Books of the Potter's Art," gives many technical details of the manufacture. Also at this time the Caffagiolo fabrique flourished under the Medici.

Francesco Maria II., who succeeded in 1574, patronized Castel Durante; at other fabriques the art declined rapidly, and his duchy passed over to the Holy See. He presented the Spezieria vases to the treasury of Loreto. Upon his death, in 1631, the art-treasures collected at Urbino were removed to Florence or dispersed. Many of the artists went to fabriques in other parts of Italy, and there was a general decline in the quality of the manufacture. A fashion for Oriental porcelain came in vogue, and attempts were made to produce it. Dr. Foresi shows that the Grand-duke Francis I. had established a private fabrique and laboratory in the Boboli Gardens, Florence, for the production of porcelain; that a record preserved notes of the composition and details of the wares made there; and that in about 1580 an artificial porcelain, the earliest known European, was produced there.

In 1763 Passeri caused a fabrique to be established at Pesaro to make porcelain, but it failed after a short existence.

Of late years there has been a revival in favor of majolica, and good work is produced in Italy to-day. Marryat and others justify the preference for Oriental porcelain over majolica, on account of its hard body and glaze. For vessels destined for constant use this preference is justified, but the adaptability of majolica to receive and develop color, and the softness and harmony resulting from this, render it admirably suited for artistic decoration.

DELLA ROBBIA WARE.

Luca della Robbia (born about 1400, died 1481), desiring to protect his terra-cotta figures by a permanent surface, invented a tin-glaze, with which he coated them; it was of better quality than previous Italian tin-glazes. His first important piece dates in 1438, and it is also the first dated piece of Italian tin-glazed ware. He also painted in vitrifiable colors on flat terra-cotta surfaces; a charming set of circular medallions, with figures representing the twelve months, painted by him in *grisaille* on a blue ground, is in existence. The colors he used were white, blue, green, maroon, and yellow.

In sculpture his style is refined and accurate; he employed the sculptors Ottaviano and Augustino to assist him. His borders of flowers are simple, his stanniferous glaze thin, almost transparent, and sometimes omitted on the flesh parts; the blue ground of his work is especially soft; his manner is broad and pure. Further characteristics are noted in the example.

Andrea della Robbia (1437-1528), who was the nephew of Luca, produced work heavier in design; the figures are short, with attenuated extremities; cherubs are frequently introduced, and he preferred fruit to flowers for the borders.

Andrea had four sons, Giovanni, Luca, Ambrosio, and Girolamo. *Giovanni* has left a signed piece marked 1521; it is mediocre. *Luca the Younger* went to Rome, and Vasari praises his work as well as that of Girolamo. *Ambrosio* is recorded as making an altar-piece. *Girolamo* made fayence *plaques* for Francis I., Château of Madrid, near Paris, which was unfortunately demolished in 1792, and the fayence broken up. He died 1567.

Antonio di Duccio, of Perugia (1459-1461), whose style resembled Luca's; *Agapito di Sassaferato*, in 1513; *Baglioni*, and *Niculoso Francisco*, of Pisa, who went to Spain, all worked in Della Robbia ware. In 1511 and 1513 *Giorgio Andreoli* executed some bass-reliefs in this style, now at Frankfort, and subsequently dishes, with figures in low-relief and lustred, were produced at his works. After 1520 the manner declined. M. Barbet de Jouy has collected many details about this ware. At Bologna, in 1870, modern copies of Luca's pieces were made.

The introduction of stanniferous enameling in Italy cannot be attributed to Luca. Twenty years before he perfected his system, *Bicci di Lorenzo* produced a glazed terra-cotta group of the Madonna and others, which still fills a lunette over the door of the Hospital of San Egidio, at Florence (*see* G. Milanesi, "Arch. St. It.," 1860). Bicci's glaze was white and opaque.

Before this, Pietro del Bono mentions the art in the "Maravita Preciosa" treatise, written in 1330; and Theophilus, in his "Div. Art. Shed." Vitruvius also mentions enameled bricks in the palace of Mausolus at Halicarnassus. An interesting notice of Luca is found in Mr. Charles Perkins's work on "Tuscan Sculptors."

Fig. 1.

DELLA ROBBIA BASS-RELIEF (Fig. 1).—A circular-headed *plaque*, with figures in low-relief, of the Virgin praying over the

Infant Jesus; above, the Father, with uplifted hands, the Holy Ghost symbolized by a dove, and six cherubim, look down upon the Mother and Child. A moulding of severe egg-pattern incloses the subject. The sky is tinted with a soft blue enamel, tinged with violet gray. The grass is colored in green and black touches. The white enamel, which appears in all other portions, is thin and fluid, thicker in some parts, presents many fine dots and occasional long shallow fissures, and also minute bubbles; a scaling off in a few spots shows partial incorporation with the body, which is buff-colored, and presents two cracks from firing. The drapery-folds are simple and charming in modeling. The varied devotional expressions, not given in this imperfect sketch, contrast with the unconscious look of the Child, and show a master-hand. It may justly be attributed to Luca. Height, twenty-six inches. (No. 7d of Signor Castellani's collection.)

TECHNICAL NOTES ON MAJOLICA AND FAYENCE.

The body of Italian fayence and majolica is a plastic clay mixed with a limy, sandy clay. It is easily scratched with an iron point. It is once baked and coated with an enamel containing lead, tin, quartz-sand, salt, and soda. This opaque enamel is then painted upon with hard fire colors, either before the second firing, as was the practice in the sixteenth century— a difficult process, but one giving great brilliancy of tone—or it is colored over the fired enamel with softer colors and fired again. Sometimes a slip of white clay is substituted to the tin enamel.

LUSTRE.—According to Piccolpasso's MS. of 1548, the lustre was produced by a *reducing* flame acting upon a lustre-pigment, which was ground in vinegar and applied thinly with a brush. The *lustre-pigment* he states to be for *ruby lustre :* terra rossa, 3; bolo arminio, 1; feretto di spagnia, 2; cinnabar, 0; and for *madreperla lustre* the quantities were respectively 6, 0, 3, 3. The pearl lustre was further ground with one *carlino* of calcined *sil-*

ver, and dissolved in a pipkin with one *quattrino* (a small *copper* coin) and red vinegar. Brongniart obtained a copper lustre by exposing pieces to oxidule of copper in a reducing atmosphere; Salvetat with azotate of oxidule of copper and carbonic-oxide gas; M. A. Fabri with iodide of iron, a little gum-arabic, and sulphate of magnesia, and a smoky atmosphere. Sulphate of iron gives a similar lustre, but less brilliant than the iodide. Brianchon and others obtain a series of faint lustres by incorporating a reducing agent, chiefly rosin and lavender-oil, with nitrate of bismuth, acetate of uranium or nickel, or salts of gold and silver, and a flux. It differs from the majolica lustres.

ANALYSES OF FAYENCE.

	Silica.	Alumina.	Lime.	Magnesia.	Iron.	Carbon. Acid and Loss.
1. Fayence of Luca della Robbia.	49.65	15.50	24.40	0.17	3.70	8.58
2. Majolica	48.00	17.50	20.12	1.17	3.75	9.46
3. Palissy fayence	67.50	28.51	1.52	0.00	2.05	0.42
4. Old Spanish fayence	46.04	18.45	17.64	0.87	3.04	13.96
5. Modern Valencia do	51.55	20.52	13.64	1.24	2.63	10.42
6. Manases fayence lustred	54.71	18.80	19.69	0.01	2.20	4.60
7. Delft fayence	49.07	16.19	18.01	0.82	2.82	13.69
8. Persian fayence	48.54	12.05	19.25	0.30	3.14	16.72
9. Nevers fayence	56.49	19.22	14.96	0.71	2.12	6.50
10. Rouen fayence	47.96	15.02	20.24	0.44	4.07	12.27
11. Paris fayence	61.50	12.99	16.24	0.15	3.01	6.10
12. Oven fayence crazed	74.90	22.10	1.60	0.50	0.70	0.20
13. Oven fayence not crazed	56.30	26.60	14.70	0.01	1.30	1.10
14. Oven fayence not crazed	55.40	29.20	13.20	0.01	0.90	1.30

Remarks.—These analyses were made after removing the enamel: 1 to 11 were analyzed at Sèvres, and are taken from Brongniart; 1 to 3 were analyzed by M. Barral. All these bodies effervesce with acid (excepting 3 and 12), showing the presence of some carbonic acid united with the lime; they are all fusible into a liquid glass, with smooth, concave fracture, of a dark-brownish yellow-green (excepting 3 and 12); the Palissy ware contains some tin in the enamel, and resembles pipe-clay; the resemblance between the Spanish and Italian fayence is notable.

De Thou states that toward 1600 a follower of the Duke of Gonzaga, from Faenza, carried the Italian fabrication to Nevers, in France. At *Nevers*, according to Brongniart, the body and glaze were formed of:

BODY : White, limy clay........	33	ENAMEL : Oxide of tin........	20
Yellow, plastic, sandy clay.	50	Oxide of lead......	80
Gray, friable, less sandy, plastic clay.........	16	Sand and some salt..	150

The firing lasted about sixteen hours. The result resembles Italian fayence. As in examples 13 and 14 the carbonate of lime in the body prevents crazing, and increases the adhesion of the enamel, it enables large, flat pieces to be made, such as the *plaque*, twenty feet by one foot eight inches, by M. Vogt. By introducing an alkaline flux, the body becomes more vitreous, also less liable to craze, but more apt to crack by changes of temperature.

INSCRIPTIONS ON ITALIAN MAJOLICA AND FAYENCE.

PROVERBIAL AND MISCELLANEOUS.—" Nemo suo sorte erat." Each one has something to grumble at.—" Non è si vago el fiore che non imbiacca o casca." There is no flower so lovely but that it fades or droops.—" Sola miseria caret invidia." Only the wretched escape envy.—" Per dormire non se acquista." Those who sleep acquire nothing.—" Basta la fede l povero se vedore." Sufficient is the faith of the poor. . . .— " Un bel morire tutta la vita onora." A beautiful death honors a lifetime.—" Suo destino ha ciascun dal di chel nasce." Each one has his destiny the day of his birth.—" Nec spe nec metu." Nor hope nor fear.—" Un bel morire è vita e gloria e fama." A beautiful death brings life, glory, and renown.—" Nemo sua sorte contentus erat." No one is contented with his fate.— " Non te fidar cogne pastore è lupo." Confide not, the shepherd is a wolf.—" Chi sta benequando piove, e ben pazzo se si muove."

—He who is well off when it rains, is a great fool if he moves.—" Cosi fugge la vita nostra." Thus life slips away (illustrated by an eel slipping through the fingers of a Cupid).—" Non ti ralegrare del mio dollo eclpelto uquaddo el mio sera voto." Do not rejoice at my pain; excepting when I myself am empty.—" Omnia P. pecuniam facta sunt." Everything is reached through money.—" Cosi na'l mondo e l'esperianza e fatta." Thus in the world experience is gained.—" Excubia. agimus. strepitus. repellimus. hostem." We watch, we watch, our watch-cries repel the enemy.—" Sura fiore." Above flowers.—" Non bene pro toto libertas venditur auro finis." Gold does not suffice everywhere to buy liberty.—" Chi lava il capo a l'asino. Se perd. o. 1556." Abbreviations of the Italian proverb, " He who washes the ass's head loses his soap and his washing."—" Aurum sitis, aurum bibe." You thirst for gold, drink gold.—" Malva per chi la tochia." The mallow-plant for him who touches her; also, by a keen play upon words, Evil comes to him who touches her.—" Solamente e ingannato chi. troppo si fida." Only the too confiding is deceived.—" E non se po mangiare senza fatigua."—For, it is known that one cannot eat without labor.—" Væ victis." Woe to the conquered!—" Asae. avanza. chi. fortuna. passa." He advances much who passes Fortune. —" Chi biena guida sua barca e sempre in porto." He who guides well his bark is always in port.—" M. che e morire che vivare co vergona." It is better to die than to live in shame.—" Tu ma qu imeve disti e te rededis ti—Nemo chonfidat mimium fechundit " (Deruta), and " Solmi sai chatt inuidex." —" Viva, viva, viva." Live, live, live.—" Seigneur, nous avons spere en toy." Lord, we have hope in thee.

HISTORICAL AND POLITICAL.—" Marco Cutio p. liberatore la patria se gitta ne la oragine." Marcus Cutius to deliver his country throws himself into the abyss.—" Come le figuli de Miobe furne saitate." How the daughters of Niobe were thunderstruck!—" David quand' uccis Gulia gigante." David when he slew Goliath the giant.—" Mutio che la sua destra erante cocie." Mutius, mistaken, burns his right hand.—" Italia mesta sotto sopra volta, come pei venti. 1540." Dejected Italy now below, now above the waves, as tossed by the wind.—"1534. Roma lasciva dal buon Carlo Quinto partita a mezza." Lascivious Rome cut in two by the good Charles V.—"Fiorenzo mesta i morti figlii piange." Disconsolate Florence weeps for her lifeless offspring (with a draped female weeping over a child; X on reverse; this may relate to the plague of 1538).— "Nero Sempe Glovi."—"Fuggie Joseppe il disonesto efeto." Joseph flies from the dishonest consequence.—"Di quercia coronato e Metillino." Coronation of Metiline with oak-leaves.— "Priamo coi figli suoi mal si consiglia."—"Cesare. abate. e. sgvizer. ala. sona."

AMATORIAL.—"Che possio fare se cossi vole amore?" What can I do if love wills it so?—"Dulce est amare." It is sweet to love.—"Per merto de mia fe in te." In reward of my faith in thee. This motto accompanies a greyhound with a heart in his mouth.—"Francesca bella a paragon di tutti." Francesca beautiful and paragon of all.—"Per fin che vivo, io sempre t'amero." As long as I live, I will always love thee.—"Penso nel mio afflito core." I ponder in my afflicted heart.... (Bisticci, or colloquial rhymes of the fifteenth and sixteenth centuries—as also the following:) "S'il dono e piccolo e di poco valore, Basta la fede, e'l povero se vedore." If the gift is small and of trifling value, my fidelity is sufficient, and my poverty is seen.—"La Madalena bella." The beautiful Magdalen.—"Non vale belezza dove sta crudelta." Beauty is worthless where cruelty exists.—"Per uso della cara sposa." For the use of the dear wife.—"Une donna presso al parto." A wife about to give birth.—"Faustina bella e pulita." Faustina beautiful and pure.—"Amor." Love.—"Oime." Woe is me. —"Co pura se." How pure you are!—"Amaro chi me amara." I will love him who will love me.—"Vivrai felice." You will live happy.—"Per merto de mia fe." In reward of my faith.— "Mariana bella sopra l'altre belle." Mariana beautiful above the other beauties.—"E sarrimo boni amici." We will be good friends.—"Omnia vincit amor." Love conquers all.—"Per amore te porto in quissta copa bella." For love I carry thee in this fine cup.—" Quista te dono per amore bella." This I give you for dear love.—" El mio core e ferito p. voe." My heart is wounded for you.—" En piu." Besides.—" O bel fiore, Amore mio bello, Amor mio caro, La Grisola, La Grisola." O beauteous flower, my fair love, my dear love, the Grisola, the Grisola.—" Memento." Remember.—" Pasa tepo." Pass, time. —" Semper vivat." Ever live.—" La vita el fue el di lo da lasera."—" Chamilla Bell Cesaria B."—" Onia vincit amor et cedamur . . . . questo." Love vanquishes all and ·. . . .—" La Bella Pollsena." The beautiful Pollsena.

SPIRITUAL AND RELIGIOUS.—" Beati qui non viderunt et criderunt." Blessed are they who have not seen and yet believe.— " Tres videt et unum adoravit." He saw three, and he adored one. The consistency of the doctrine of the Trinity condensed. —" Non recuso il morir pe. C.' altri viver." I do not refuse to die, provided another may live.—" Chi servi Dio con purita di core vive contento e poi salvato muore." Who serves God with purity of heart, lives contented and can die saved.—" Virtus in atione consiste." Virtue in actions consists.—" Homo pronobit et Deus disponi." Man proposes and God disposes. —" Ardet eternum." Eternal fire.—" Viva, viva in eternum." Live, live in eternity.—" Ama Dio." Love God.—" Pensa a Dios." Think of God.—" Ecce Agnus Dei." Here is the Lamb of God.—" Iv. II. Pon. Max. Tu. es. sacerdos. i. eter." Julius II., Pontifex Maximus, thou art priest eternally.—" Justitia Dedio." The justice of God.—" Timete. Dominum." Fear God.—" Libera. me. domine. ab. homine. malo. et. a. lingua. iniusta." Deliver me, O God, from the evil of man and an unjust tongue !—" Quant ac rup ieta."—" Pensa el fine." Think of the end.—" Per Dio." For God.—" Fides onia."—" Timor domini sui e filium suum." The fear of God and of his Son.— " Ispera Dio." Hope in God.—" Spes mea in Deo est. Domine mento mei. 1521." My hope is in God. May God remember me !—" Gloria in eselsis Deo et in Terra Pax." Glory to God in the highest, and peace on earth !—" Avendo. io. iobe. doe.

amalate. in. chasa. merecomandae. aquista. gloriosa. ver. maria. ef. sao." On a votive disk.

MYTHOLOGICAL.—" La Dea delle tartarie porte." The Goddess of the Gates of Tartarus (Proserpine).—" Del parnasso l' monte D'Ovidio, al libro V. 1544." The Mount Parnassus of Ovid, Book V.—" Il vano Amante de sua propria inmago." The vain lover of his own image (Narcissus).—" Alfeo ch' segue sua diua Aretusa." Alpheus who follows his divine Arethusa.—" Angelica ligata al duro scoglio." Angelica bound to the hard rock.—" Come Apollo tolse la vaca a Argano." How Apollo seized the Vaca at Argos.—" Giove mutato in tore et Europa." Jove changed into a bull and Europa.—" Hercole amazzo Lydra." Hercules slaying the Hydra. —" D'Alcione la vision tremenda e vera." The fearful and true vision of Alcion.—" Mostra Candauli. Re sua donna a Gigia."—" Narcisso mutato in Fiore." Narcissus changed to a flower.—" Plutone quando rapi Proserpina." Pluto when he snatched away Proserpine.

PHARMACEUTICAL (of interest in the History of Medicine). —DI ANISI — V . BIAE . CAF — VERA . PRIGRA . G — LOC . SAVM . EXPE . — SY . DE . NENVFARI . 1507 — SYR . DE . CALAMET . 1507 — DIA . CODION . 1507 — DIA . PRUNI . SIMPLEX — CATARTICO . IMP . 1507 — COFETIQ . AMECH — ZVCAO . BVCALOSAO. 1507 — LOC . DE . PAPAVERO 1507 — ZVCCARVM . ROSATUM — DIA . IRRIS — SXo . DE FLORIB . P. SICOR — SYo . D . INF . VOSAR — ZVCCARO . ROSATO — SVSINA . AROMATI — LISSIVA . SIMPLI — ANFRV . . . . INCENSO — SVCCINE . AMASSINE — VIVOLE — A . DE . GRAMINIS — A . APIIT — A . LATVCE — O . D . SCORPIONE — S . D . MENTA — EL . D . BACI . LAVRI — YSOPOHAMIDO — SY . DE . QM . INEVVIO . RVM — CONSVA . V — M — CONSERVE DACHORI — HENALBO — OLIO ; VOLPIN — SIR . DI . CEDRO — SYo , HIFDUTINI — SYo . DAHFCITIO — SPo . DIBISANTI — CONS : D'AFFENZ — CONS . DI . GRUGNIAL — ENGLOSA

RODIX — PERTARLIO . ODIF — MOSTARDA . F . —
DIA . CATHOLICN . M — DIA . CALAMENTO — DIA :
SENA . NICOL — ZAFARANO — V . MORDIFICHAT —
A . DE . CAMOMELA — A . DE . EOFRAGA — A .
DMATRICHA — A . ENFRAGIA — A . CAPILLOR . NE
— ISOPUS . HUMIDA — A . CDIGARD . STELLAT .
1689 —

THE VENETIAN STATES.

History.—The *Veneti*, a people of uncertain origin, were invaded by the Gauls in 350 B. C. The Romans gradually acquired the country, and founded Aquileia, 181 B. C. Venice was founded by families fleeing from Aquileia and Padua before Attila in 452 A. D. It was governed from A. D. 697 to 1797 by one hundred and twenty-two doges, including the first doge, Anafesto Paululio, and the last, Luigi Manin. During this period Venice becomes independent of the Eastern Empire, A. D. 997; her commerce increases; she acquires Dalmatia and Istria. The Venetians ravage the Greek Archipelago, 1125; aid the crusaders, 1202; make war upon Genoa in 1293, and again in 1350 and 1377; conquer Padua and Verona, 1404; Brescia and Bergamo, 1428; Ravenna, 1454; Athens, 1466; Cyprus, 1475; and in 1501 take Faenza and Rimini, which were also pottery centres. The discovery of America and the passage to India injures Venetian commerce. From 1508 to 1739 the Venetians engage in wars against the Turks. In 1797 Bonaparte divides Venetia, giving part to Austria and part to the Italian republics; with various changes Venice reverts, in 1867, to the kingdom of Italy.

VENICE produced enameled wares of artistic merit as early as in the latter half of the fifteenth century, as is shown by the costumes and inscriptions in Venetian dialect on some vases. The archives of Modena show that, in 1520, Titian superintended the execution of an order for Murano glass and majolica vases for the pharmacy of Duke Alfonso I. His agent, Tebaldo, wrote to him as follows: " By the boatman, John

Tressa, I send to your excellency eleven large vases and eleven medium vases, and twenty small, in majolica, with the covers ordered by Titian, for the pharmacy of your excellency."

A fayence pavement, in the sacristy of St. Elena, bearing the arms of the Giustiniani family, with the dates 1450 and 1480, and one dated 1510, in the church of St. Sebastian, bearing the crown of the Lando family, are attributed to Venetian artists. Venetian pieces are known dated 1540 and 1542. The fabrique of Mo. Ludovico produced fine wares. In the Brunswick collection are samples of such, dated 1546 and 1568, the latter inscribed *Zener Domenico da Venetia feci in la botega al ponte sito del andar a San Polo*. Pieces marked with an anchor, one dated 1571, another, by Louis-Denis Marini, 1636, are probably Venetian, as the anchor-mark is found later on Venetian porcelain.

A letter is known, sent by Mo. Battista di Franceso, of Murano, near Venice, to the Duke of Ferrara, in 1567, in which he styles himself *maestro in majolica, and manufacturer of vases very noble, rare, very beautiful, and various*, and asks for a loan of three hundred ducats to enable him to transfer his manufacture to Ferrara.

Characteristics.—The body of the sixteenth-century Venetian ware is buff-colored and close, the glaze even and grayish. The designs were traced in blue, shaded in blue, and heightened with white. The reverse of the dishes is variously marked with sprays around the rim, and radiating lines near the centre, a mark also found upon Paduan ware. Oak-leaves are frequently used in the decoration, which is usually fully distributed over the ware, and fertility of conception is displayed. The Renaissance style prevails in the sixteenth century. Later pieces reproduce designs seen on textile stuffs of the seventeenth century. Some are coarsely done. In the eighteenth century Venice produced wares highly fired, thin, close, sonorous, with floral ornaments in low-relief, with a preponderance of blue and brown on a light-blue or whitish-gray ground. A bright iron red, also seen on Venetian porcelain, is found on later pieces.

Among subjects found on fayence attributed to Venice are: A small trophy of arms surrounded by a wide border of oak-branches, masks, fruit, etc., in pale blue on a gray ground; a half-figure of Diana between the letters V. B., and wide border of strap-work interlaced and cornucopia, masks, and cherubs' heads; a plateau with medallions bearing portraits of Semiramis, Portia, Zenobia, Fulvia—on reverse, 13 *di Aprille* 1543 Aolasdinr; a Cupid running with a basket of flowers; radiating palmette ornament; a youth stooping to stir a blazing fire; trophies, etc., among which are figures of Plenty, and Cupid with a dog; a mask of a satyr carrying a basket of fruit; trophy of a helmet, a shield, and a triple pipe; a nude boy standing and holding a bunch of leaves; a boy attired with a scarf, plucking a flower; on a book is the date 1557; a drug-pot, *dia fena nicol*, with leafage, and a shield of arms, signed by Jacomo; two men beneath a large archway.

In the Museo Correr, at Venice, are seventeen beautiful pieces, ascribed to a Faenza manufactory; one is dated 1482. The subjects are: "Solomon adoring the Idols;" "Solomon with Bathsheba and Adonijah;" "The Four Seasons;" "Narcissus and Echo;" "Marsyas and Apollo;" "Midas crowned;" "Peleus and Thetis;" "Meleager;" "Julia and Otinelo," an old Italian romance; "Young Lady caressing a Unicorn," young cavalier before her; "Eurydice and Aristæus;" "Orpheus playing;" "Charon in a Boat;" "Orpheus and Eurydice;" "Orpheus and the Brutes;" "Orpheus and Bacchante;" "A Bearded Man in the Costume of the Early Sixteenth Century," his hands chained.

TREVISO produced at first inferior and inartistic wares which Garzoni mentions as much inferior to Faenza. A bowl is known signed Don Parisi a Travisio, dated 1538, ornamented outside with arabesques on blue, inside with a subject. "The Sermon on the Mount," and underneath with a portrait. Later, pieces in the style of Moustier, and in 1769 common *graffiti*, are made.

BASSANO.—Simone Marinoni founded the Bassano manufactory in about 1540. A piece dated 1555 is inferior technically. Later, and at the beginning of the seventeenth century, this fabrique produced excellent pieces decorated with landscapes after the Venetian painters. A plate exists signed *Antonio Terchi in Bassano*, and marked with a five-pointed crown, open or uncovered at the top; another with the same mark, and *Bo Terchy Bassano*. The crown is found elsewhere, and the Terchi worked at other places.

NOVE.—A fabrique was established at Nove, near Bassano, by the Antonibon, at the end of the seventeenth century, which produced admirable work about 1750. The surface is pure and white, and the painting good.

PADUA.—In the remains of a manufactory at Padua was found a disk twenty-one inches in diameter, with a Madonna between St. Roch and St. Lucy, in relief thinly enameled; it is signed Nicoleti, and is after a cartoon of Nicolo Pizzolo, of the time of Mantegna. Other pieces inscribed Padua are dated 1548, 1564, 1565. The wares of this time resemble the inferior quality of Venetian. The glaze is of a blue-gray tint; the designs are coarse and roughly colored. Pharmacy vases with two handles, decorated with arabesques, flowers, and grotesques on a pearl-gray ground, are called *alla padovana*.

CANDIANA.—There are evidences that fayence was long made at this manufactory, and at an early date; the locality is near Padua. The style of pieces dated in the seventeenth century and marked Candiana is a poor imitation of the Syrian and Rhodian wares in Persian manner. One piece bears S. F. C. on the reverse; others *MS. Dega* and *Pa. Crosa* on the face.

VERONA possessed a manufactory, of which a well-painted *istoriati*, dated 1563, is known.

LOMBARDY.

The *Lombards* or *Longobards* came from Scandinavia by way of the Danube and Pannonia, A. D. 548, where they remained forty-two years. Justinian or Narses called them to Italy, where they seized Verona, Milan (569), Pavia, and Umbria (573), and reigned there until their last king, Didier, Duke of Brescia, was overturned by Charlemagne, A. D. 774, who conferred the vacant fiefs on his own chiefs, and confirmed the others in the possession of their previous chiefs, provided they swore obeisance to him.

In 1167 the first Lombard league of Milan, Venice, Padua, and Mantua, was formed to repel the German Empire. In 1183 they defeated Frederick Barbarossa. In 1226 they formed a second league against Frederick II. Later, petty tyrants and dissensions arose, and the German and French sovereigns disputed for it from the fifteenth century till 1859, when the French gave it to the King of Sardinia.

MILAN, in the middle of the eighteenth century, produced fayence in imitation of the Chinese style, somewhat like Delft and Dresden china, and frequently gilded. But pieces exist, painted with bouquets in the style of the seventeenth-century textile fabrics, and inscribed *Milao*. Others, with Watteau figures, are signed *Milano*. Another piece bears *F di Pasquale Rubati Milo*, and others are marked P. R., and *Mro Brecchi*.

LODI.—A piece is known signed *Ferret Lodi ;* another with the monogram M. A., *Lodi*, 1764. Ignazio Cavazzuti, in 1790, directed a manufactory at Lodi. The Lodi fayence resembles that of Treviso, with Hindoo and Chinese figures.

SARDINIA.

TURIN.—Savoy possessed a manufactory in 1564 under the government of Emmanuel Philibert.

There is a piece covered with a thick and very white enamel inscribed *Fatta in Torino adi* 12 *de Setebre* 1577. Others bear the Sardinian cross and the crown of Victor Amadeus II., or Charles Emmanuel III., who succeeded to the throne in 1675 and 1730.

Later pieces with the same shield are inscribed *Fabrica Reale di Torino*, 1737, and *Gratapaglia fe. Taur.*

LAFOREST.—A piece is known inscribed *Laforest en Savoye*, 1752.

STATES OF GENOA.

GENOA.—A manufactory existed there in the sixteenth century. Piccolpasso mentions the wares of Genoa ornamented like those of Venice. The later pieces in the seventeenth century bear the mark of a lighthouse with hanging beacon.

SAVONA.—A pottery existed at this sea-side town in 1576, which took a large development in the seventeenth century; the wares have more a commercial character than of good art.

The body of the Savona ware is thin and well fired, and the decoration usually in blue upon bluish white; the glaze is good. The principal mark is the shield of arms of the town, surmounted with a crown.

Girolamo Salomini, about 1650, who signed G. S., and with the star of Solomon; Gian Antonio Guidobono, and his sons Bartolomeo and Domenico; Gian Tomasso Torteroli; Agostino Ratti, about 1720; and Jacques Borelly, in 1799, worked at Savona.

At the present day Savona produces ordinary work in glazed and unglazed terra-cotta.

ARBISOLA had a manufactory, resembling mostly the later Savona in character. There exists a picture of the Nativity on tiles, inscribed *Arbissolo*, and signed *Gerolamo*, 1576, resembling the signature of Gerolamo d'Urbino.

NORTHERN DUCHIES.

FERRARA.—The Marquis Campori has studied this group, and shows that artists of Faenza carried their manufacture to Ferrara, beginning with a mention of painted and glazed pieces in 1443, and of one Melchior in 1495. Biagio of Faenza is mentioned as being in the service of Alfonso I., Duke of Ferrara, in 1501 and 1506. In 1510 Pope Julius II. took from Alfonso I. part of his possessions; Alfonso, being obliged to retrench, sold his jewels, and began using pottery vessels of his own manufacture. In 1522 Antonio of Faenza, and in 1528 Cato of Faenza, were in charge of the manufacture. About this time the artists Camillo, the Dossi, and Baptiste are recorded. The brothers Dossi also decorated in fresco the palaces of Alfonso of Este, in the Raffaelesque manner. Besides the above manufactory subventioned by Alfonso I., his brother, Sigismond of Este, protected another fabrique located in the Schifanoia Palace, under the direction of Biagio Biasini of Faenza, mentioned in the archives from 1513 to 1524; the artists El Frate, Grosso, and Zaffarino, worked there in 1523.

In 1534 to 1559, during the reign of Hercules II., the archives only show Peter Paul Stanghi, of Faenza, as working there. On the accession of Alfonso II., a change in style is noted from that of Faenza to the Urbino manner, and the names of Camillo of Urbino, and his brother Battista, appear in the archives.

Alfonso I., about 1504, had caused laboratory experiments to be made, resulting in the production of the *bianco allatato*, or milky-white glaze, and Alfonso II., who continued the experiments, succeeded, about 1567, in making porcelain, according to a letter sent to Florence by Bernardo Canigiani, Florentine embassador at Ferrara, but no pieces of this ware have been found, while the porcelain of Florence is well known.

In 1579 Alfonso II., on the occasion of his marriage with Marguerite of Gonzaga, had a service made, painted with a flaming pyre, under the device *Ardet Æternum*, which is also found upon his medals. Upon his death in 1597 his dukedom was absorbed by the states of the Church. A piece painted in manganese on white is signed *Thomas Masselli Ferrarien.*

Characteristics.—The peculiar brilliant, white glaze, called *Bianco di Ferrara*, is mentioned by Piccolpasso as being used there. Grotesque decoration upon white is met with. The arms of Gonzaga and Este are seen on a piece, probably made when John Francis II. married Elizabeth, sister of Alfonso I.

MODENA.—In 1472 Enrico, and in 1489 Gio da Modena,

are recorded as potters. In the sixteenth century Cristoforo da Modena is mentioned a *boccalaro*, and Piccolpasso speaks of the fabrique of Modena. C. and D. A. Rubbiani make fayence there at the present time.

REGGIO possessed a fabrique in 1565, and SCANDIANA one in 1754.

SASSUOLO.—Gio Andrea Ferrari founded a manufactory there in 1741, to which the almost exclusive monopoly of the duchy was granted by the Duke Francesco III. He was joined by Gio Maria Dallari, and obtained later a complete monopoly. The products were exported, but no artists of note appear to have been connected with the fabrique. However, Pietro Lei and Ignace Cavatuzzi are known.

MANTUA.—About 1450 fayence of a probably inferior quality was made here, as shown by the archives.

TUSCANY.

Etruria or *Tuscia* may have been colonized by the Lydians, according to Herodotus. The Romans, who attacked Etruria in the fourth century B. C., and took possession of it 265 B. C., derived many of their laws and superstitions from the Etruscans. The present Tuscany was formerly a grand-duchy in Etruria. It formed part of the Lombard kingdom when Charlemagne conquered it in 774 A. D., and later broke up into the republics of Florence, Pisa, Sienna, Lucca, etc. Florence became the chief of these under the Medici in 1251, who became the restorers of fine arts and literature in Italy. Cosmo was chief of the Florentine Republic in 1434; Lorenzo the Magnificent ruled 1469-1492; his son, Giovanni de' Medici, became Pope Leo X.; Catherine de' Medici became Queen of France, 1547. In 1531 Alexander I. was the first duke of the Medici. In 1537 Duke Cosmo I. followed, and was created hereditary grand-duke by the pope in 1569. The succeeding Medici grand-dukes were, in 1574, Francis I.; 1578, Ferdinand I.; 1608, Cosmo II.; 1670, Cosmo III.; 1723, John Gaston was the last of

CAFFAGIOLO. 45

the Medici. In 1737 came Francis II., Duke of Lorraine, who became later Emperor of Germany. In 1765 Leopold I. followed, who became emperor 1790; and his successor, Ferdinand III., was expelled by the French, when, during 1801 to 1807, Bonaparte reëstablished the kingdom of Etruria, but in 1814 Ferdinand III. was restored.

UNKNOWN FABRIQUE.—Certain pieces of mezza-ware bear a close resemblance to each other, and evidences of a Tuscan origin, probably of 1450-1480. In some a decoration of peacocks' feathers is frequent. · The earliest dated piece is a tin-glazed figure of the Virgin and Child enthroned in a niche, marked 1477.

Certain pieces decorated in pale blue and yellow, upon a good white ground, are also attributed to a Tuscan fabrique unknown.

CAFFAGIOLO.—Cosmo I. established in a castle at this place, situated between Florence and Bologna, a fabrique of earthenware.

Characteristics.—The glaze is rich, even, and purely white; a very dark cobalt-blue of great intensity is used chiefly for grounds, and laid on with a coarse brush in apparent strokes. A bright yellow; a brilliant opaque, and unique orange not found elsewhere; a peculiar, semi-transparent, liquid copper-green; an opaque, bright Indian red; also brown and purple, are used. The Siena wares are somewhat similar. Grotesques and *a candeliere* decoration are frequent; the drawing is bold and firm, and the figures frequently outlined with a narrow blue line. Florentine coats of arms, notably the Medici arms and mottoes, constantly occur, and the letters S. P. Q. F. for *Senatus Populusque Florentinus.* Among other coats of arms on Caffagiolo wares are those of the Rinuccini and Pazzi families; the arms of Leo X., with the motto *Sempe Glovi ;* those of Ferdinand I., Grand-duke of Tuscany; and Medici impaling Lorraine.

The name of the place is written on the reverse in many ways, as Caffagiulo, Cafagiol, Chaffagiolo, Chafaggilolo, Gafagizotto, etc. Among the dates inscribed are 1507, 1509, 1514, 1541, 1544, 1546, 1547, 1570, 1590.

The name of the artist Benedetto Bocchi, of the period 1640, appears on one piece, while the following artists are known to have worked there: Giacomo Ridolfi, Loys Ridolfi, Flaminio Fontana, and Pietro da Cortona.

The name Andrea di Bono, probably that of the owner, appears on a piece dated 1491.

A monogram formed of P and S, or of those letters with an L, distinguishes many Caffagiolo pieces.

The earlier pieces are enameled, some only on one face, with borders in antique style, and the drawing has something of the primitive aspect of fourteenth-century woodcuts; the nimbus of the saints is exaggerated in size; the drapery is crinkled, and at first blue only is used.

The fifteenth century shows progress, but not until the sixteenth century does the full harmony of varied colors appear; the family arms are colored in yellow for gold, tin enamel for silver, a rich red, and azure blue, as seen on pieces dated 1507 and 1509.

A golden lustre, with the Medici arms and the P S monogram, appears on one piece, and a few other lustred pieces are known, all of the sixteenth century, and subsequent to the first use of varied colors.

Some pieces show great artistic merit. A dependent fabrique seems to have existed at Galiano, for on a piece bearing the P S mark is the inscription *In Galiano nellanno*, 1547.

Some of the subjects on Caffagiolo pieces are as follows: The Triumph of Justice; Hercules, accompanied by mounted knights, precedes a four-wheeled golden car drawn by youths, which supports a throne formed of dolphins, on which sits Justice; below the throne are two bearded, long-haired men holding each a sceptre and a book. Cupid blindfolded bound to a column supported by four boy musicians, and a sphinx and harpy on either side; beneath lies the sea with dolphins and children. A Medusa head, with margin of three bombards discharging shells, and a shield of arms. A central shield of arms carried by three Cupids, with side medallions representing grape gathering, treading, and ploughing, and a Medusa head. Alexander meeting Diogenes, in the manner of Luca Signorelli. An equestrian figure spearing a dragon, of about 1510. Four soldiers conversing, in Italian costumes. A procession of a cavalier mounted on an elephant, followed by halberdiers, cardinals on

FIG. 2.

mules, ecclesiastics, Pope Leo X. in a palanquin, pikemen, and standard-bearers, with the Medici arms on the standards. A triumphal procession, after Mantegna, with lictors, fasces, a jester, musicians with harp and guitar, followed by horses harnessed. This dish formed one of a series representing the procession, dated 1514. Vulcan forging a wing for Cupid, in an Italian landscape. St. George, after the statue of Donatello. An infant falling head foremost from a tree. Apollo and Pan, a shepherd, a satyr, and two crowned monks. A celebrated plate of about 1520, representing a majolica painter painting the border of a *tondino* in the presence of two visitors; one of the visitors holds a cloth and a fruit, which appear to serve as a model for the artist's border. Two brushes and a separate cup are represented for each color.

HERALDIC SHIELD (Fig. 2).—A cock standing with *fleur-*

FIG. 3.

de-lis in his beak. Date, 1466, on the face. Outline traced in black, filled in with black, except the thighs, which are violet gray, and the beak, feet, and outline of gills, which are yellow; black border. The date of this piece is nine years earlier than a piece of similar ware in the Cluny Museum. The white enamel is thick and warmer in tone than the Della Robbia enamel. The shape of the piece is that of an heraldic shield. Height, thirteen inches. No. 8. Attributed to Caffagiolo.

ALBARELLO (Fig. 3).—Two men sawing off the horns of a goat. The inscription, in blue—TIRA TIRA COMPAGNO MIO CHE CHINE SCAMPA FIGLIOLO DE DIO, which reads, " Draw, draw, my companion; he who escapes it (the horn) is," etc.—is in a spirit of satire, savoring of the Reformation. The contents may have been aperient, as the label bears DIA CODION—that is, "through horn." An interlaced pattern of yellow rings, the whole upon a dark-blue ground, is inclosed with a wreath of green leaves. The men have or-

FIG. 4.

ange jackets, yellow trousers, and turquoise stockings. The buff body of the vase is not enameled at the base. This drug-pot belongs to the same set as the following. Height, nine inches. Caffagiolo. No. 34. The set is dated 1507.

ALBARELLO (Fig. 4).—Head of a pope with tiara, and a

dolphin seizing each shoulder. The label bears LOC DE PAPAVRO, which signifies equally "Syrup of Poppies," or "Syrup of the true Pope." Below dogs have set upon a stag. Ground, dark blue : a wreath of green leaves, yellow pears, tied with turquoise ribbon. A spirit of satire is visible. Dated 1507; height nine inches. Caffagiolo. No. 39.

DEEP DISH (Fig. 5).—Madonna with cross, praying, surrounded by six cherubs, traced in blue filled in with yellow, in a sky blue with orange clouds. Below a walled city, and trees

FIG. 5.

in blue, except one with larger leaves in green. A rich border of cornucopias and Renaissance scrolls, outlined in blue, upon an orange ground, and shaded in blue, thick copper-green, and brown. Caffagiolo. Diameter, sixteen and one-half inches. No. 39c. Only a portion of the border is shown in the sketch.

Among subjects in Signor Castellani's collection attributed to Caffagiolo are: "A Youth crowned;" "Laura B——;" "Iabina;" "Orsini Arms;" "Child kneeling before a Skull," and motto, *Memento mei;* "Cupid riding on his Bow;" *Semper vivat.*

SIENA.—This republic was subjected by the Emperor Charles V., and in 1555 given to his son, who ceded it to Cosmo of Tuscany in 1557. It was incorporated in France from 1808 to 1814. A considerable number of pieces of Siena pottery are known.

Characteristics.—The work is notable for exquisite finish, and bears a general resemblance to Caffagiolo decoration. *Bianco sopra Bianco* ornament was much used, and *coppa amatoria* were made there.

A pavement of four hundred and seventy-two fayence tiles, dated 1509, has been found in the Petrucci Palace at Siena; the border is beautifully painted with grotesques and figures of children, in various tints, on a black ground, in a style much used at Siena.

A clever artist worked there in 1510, believed to be Maestro Benedetto; inscribed on the reverse of a piece representing St. Jerome in the desert, painted in blue, is, *Fata i Siena da Mo. Benedetto.* The pieces marked I. P. and F. O. I. are attributed to this Benedetto, on account of the similarity of treatment and handling. Much later, Ferdinando Maria Campani, in 1733, executed at Siena work of some general merit and excellent in design; he has left pieces also dated 1736 and 1747; his subjects are usually mythological.

Bor. Terchi Romano worked at Siena in 1727. The arms of the Piccolomini and of the Petrucci families are found on Siena ware.

At the present day Signor Pepi, in Siena, makes tiles and plates fairly copied from the old.

A bass-relief of "The Entombment," of the Della Robbia school, is inscribed *Fre Bernardinus de Siena in B. S. Satus.*

The following are some of the subjects on pieces from

Siena, or attributed to it: St. James the Great, in a landscape, a fine piece; Abraham about to sacrifice Isaac, about 1510; St. Sebastian bound to a tree; medallion figure of the infant St. John; *amatoria*, with Cupid riding on a snail and playing a flute, border with phœnix, pelican, pierced heart, and heart with motto *Amore;* an old man seated contemplating a skull held in his right hand, signed by Mo. Benedetto; the centaur Nessus carrying off Dejanira; a female figure with a unicorn; mailed knights fighting for a prisoner. The following pieces are by Capmany, about 1747: Nymphs grooming Pegasus, from an antique painting in Bartoli; Galatea, after A. Caracci; dance of the Graces; Mercury and Paris; the temptation, after Raffaele; Juno soliciting Æolus to let loose the winds. In Signor Castellani's collection is the figure of a woman, with border of trophies, and S. P. Q. R.

PISA.—Pisa was founded about 600 B. C., became subject to Florence in 1405, and independent again in 1494. It was retaken by the Florentines in 1509. A university founded there in 1343 was revived by the Medici in 1472 and in 1542.

Fayence is believed to have been made at Pisa, and exported, in the twelfth, thirteenth, and fourteenth centuries, judging from allusions by contemporary writers. The *bacini*, which decorated the outer walls of Pisan churches, are by some attributed to Pisa.

There is a fine vase ornamented with grotesques on white ground in the Urbino style, and inscribed *Pisa* in two cartouches on the sides; the white ground is less glossy than that of Urbino, which is lead-glazed.

FLORENCE.—Florence first comes into notice when founded by the soldiers of Sylla, B. C. 80. It was destroyed by Totila, A. D. 541. Charlemagne rebuilt it in 800. In 1198 Florence formed an independent republic, or civic democracy; in 1266 the *arti*, or trades' guilds, were established, which were represented by *consoli*, or deputies, who passed resolutions which the *signoria*, or executive government, carried out. In 1265 Dante was born there. In 1582 the *Academia della Crusca* was founded;

it was so called because, while it enriched literature, it rejected, like bran (*crusca*), all words not purely Tuscan.

. Nothing is known of a fayence fabrique at Florence, although Lazari remarks that Flaminio Fontana was invited to Florence by Francis de' Medici, and remained there several years decorating vases in the Urbino style.

Francis I. (1574-1587) established at his castle of San Marco a laboratory, where the first-known European porcelain was produced from Vicenza kaolin, and an artificial fritted mass to which we have already alluded; the pieces were merely experimental, and the manufacture was not continued. A record kept in the laboratory shows the composition used.

The decoration is either in grotesques with coats of arms, some having for a mark initials of the words *Franciscus Medici Magnus Etruriæ dux secundus*, or in semi-Oriental style, marked with the cupola of Santa Maria and the letter F.

Many other attempts were made in Italy at about that time to make porcelain. Signor Castellani exhibits two interesting pieces of Medicean porcelain: one a fluted basin, with blue *camaïeu*, representing St. Mark, with a glory, seated writing; near him the lion holds a tablet inscribed with a monogram, perhaps that of Giulio Romano, or Giulio Pepi: the other a plate decorated in Chinese style, marked with the dome and F, and some floral figures in blue. The blue is faint and grayish. The color of the body is white, slightly tinged with gray, green, and blue. The glaze is moderately glossy.

ASCIANO.—At this place Luca della Robbia found a kiln which enabled him to fire a piece that he had painted for the church Dei Minori Conventuali, representing the Virgin, the angel Raphael, the young Toby, and St. Anthony.

MONTE LUPO.—There are pieces dated Monte Lupo, 1627, 1632, 1663; one inscribed *Raffaele Girolamo fecit Mte. Lupo*, 1639, rudely painted.

The body is a bright-red clay and glazed with manganese brown, with white-slip arabesque and floral ornaments, and some in imitation of gilding. Other pieces are in the usual Italian style, but coarse and rudely designed; one such is inscribed *Dipinto Giovinale Tereni da Montelupo.* The signature of *Diacinto Mori* is also met. Some pieces painted over the glaze with oil-colors which are not fired, are seen.

SAN QUIRIGO.—Cardinal Chigi, desiring to revive the old majolica, established a fabrique here in 1714, the products of which he gave away as presents. Pienzentelli, a painter who had studied the style of Fontana, and after him Giovanni Terchi, and Ferd. Maria Campani, directed the work.

BORGO SAN SEPOLCRO.—A curious lamp, mounted in silver, and decorated with flowers and drapery, is inscribed *Citta Borgo S. Sepolcro—a 6 febrajo* 1771—*Mart. Rioletus fecit.*

DUCHIES OF URBINO.

PESARO.—Tomasso Garzoni, a Venetian nobleman, who wrote in 1585, praises the workmanship of the Pesaro pottery, while he mentions that of Faenza for its whiteness and delicacy. Passeri, who wrote in 1750, describes the glazed and enameled pottery at Pesaro, beginning in 1502, and ascribes the early lustred *bacili* to Pesaro, while a document in 1510 enumerates *majolica* as one of the trades of Pesaro.

Passeri mentions a partnership in 1462 between Mastro Simone da Siena di casa Piccolomini and Matteo di Raniere da Cagli, for enlarging a pottery in Pesaro.

In 1486 a decree of John Sforza of Aragon, Count of Pesaro, prohibits the importation of foreign pottery into his county. In 1567 Guidobaldo issued an edict in favor of Jacomo Lanfranco for his discovery of a method of applying true gold upon earthenware, but what this method was is not now known.

Characteristics.—It is probable that the use of various colors preceded the lustre at Pesaro. The early style is known by its lustre and blue; the figures are drawn in an archaic style of great breadth, with large veils and free and ample folds in the drapery. Although the manner is good, the execution is primitive and stiff. The decoration is often Persian in taste. There are usually no fabrique-marks. After the accession of

Guidobaldo II., in 1538, a distinct change occurs, and compositions adapted from the great masters are introduced. The *Lanfranchi* fabrique made chiefly *istoriati* pieces in the sixteenth century.

The dates of 1502, 1540, 1541, 1542, 1545, 1552, 1566, appear; after 1560 the art declined.

From inscriptions and other evidence it is known that fabriques named as follows existed at Pesaro: Mastro Gironimo, Vasaro; Mastro Baldassar, Vasaro; Mastro Matteo, Bocalaro; Mastro Girolamo di Lanfranco delle Gabice, 1542; Alfonzo Marzi, 1718; Giuseppe Bertolucci and Francesco di Fattori, in 1757; Antonia Casali and F. A. Caligari, in 1763. The artist-names of Terencio, Iacomo Pinsur, or I. P., and Pietro Lei of Saffuolo, in 1763, are found on some pieces; also the arms of Cardinal Pucci.

The arms found upon wares are those of the first owners and donors. This appears in a letter of Lorenzo the Magnificent to Roberto Malatesta, thanking him for a present of decorated pieces, saying, "They please me entirely by their perfection and rarity, being quite novelties in these parts, and are valued more than if of silver, the donor's arms serving daily to recall their origin."

Coppa Amatoria and half-length portraits of women, with the addition of *Bella* after the name, are numerous. Among the lustred pieces are the portraits of Louis d'Armagnac, Duke de Némours, in 1477 to 1503, of the Sforza princes, and shields of Dauphiny and Burgundy, and of Popes Leo X. and Clement VII. de' Medici, showing the lustre to have been used for more than a century.

The yellow-lustre pigment of Pesaro is of great beauty, and, when laid over blue, shows by reflected light red, golden, green, and blue rays, more brilliant than the lustre of Diruta. The later Caligari and Casali style is an inferior imitation of Sèvres.

At the present day Benucci and Latti, at Pesaro, make lustred ware resembling the early Pesaro pieces; the lustre is more brassy and less nacreous than the old.

PESARO.

Among subjects on Pesaro ware, surrounded by decorative borders, are: A lion roaring, a branch of foliage behind him; an equestrian figure galloping, lance in hand; Mutius Scævola burning his hand before Porsena; Lucretia stabbing herself before the citizens of Rome; Mars and Venus; the finding of Moses; Jupiter and Europa in an interior; Hercules slaying Cacus; Jason; Narcissus; the birth of Adonis; the Virgin and St. John standing near the cross, with the scroll, crown of thorns, and the nails; Horace alone defending his country against all Tuscany, 1541. In Signor Castellani's collection

FIG. 6.

are: Bust of *La romana bella;* arms of Pope Paul III.; St. Peter; *Francesca; Falsirone;* Imp. Adrianus Cæsar Aug.; the vision of Astyages, 1546; Actæon chased by his dogs; *Vulcano. ala. Fucina.* 1549; and the cups shown in Figs. 6 and 7.

CUP ON STAND (Fig. 6).—Bust, profile-portrait of young

man, with scroll, inscribed *Curtio*. The flesh and scroll are shaded in yellow. The glaze is crackled. Hair auburn red; hat Vandyck brown; outlines, also cloak, in dark olive-green; sleeves reddish brown; rim yellow; shirt whitish. Unlustred. Attributed to Pesaro. Diameter nine inches. No. 245.

CUP ON STAND (Fig. 7).—Bust, profile-portrait of young woman, with scroll, inscribed *Silvia Diua*, 1524, or "Silvia, goddess," so called. Outlined in blue; flesh shaded with ochre

FIG. 7.

hatchings; scarf deeper ochre; dress yellow brown, sleeves green; chemise white, with blue design and knotted sleeve; hair shaded in long blue lines, tinted yellow ochre, bound by green ribbon shaded in blue and ochre; ground deep dark blue; eye in two shades of blue. *Bianco fisso* used for lights of flesh and linen. Blue letters and shading on scroll. Ochre rim. Unlustred. Attributed to Pesaro. Diameter eight and a half inches. No. 246.

CASTEL DURANTE, *later named* URBANIA.—A potter, Giovanni dei Bistugi, is spoken of in the archives in 1361. In the year 1363 the name of Maestro Gentile appears as supplying the court with fayence. A pottery existing near there in 1364 is also mentioned, and allusions to this manufacture are made in documents of 1461, 1480, and 1495. Over the entrance of a house, built at Castel Durante in 1440, are the arms of the Feltreschi, consisting of three bars, with the eagle of Ferretrana in relief, a crowned griffon as crest, and the inscription *Ospes Ciccus Gattus salvere te jubet.*

A piece dated 1508, Castel Durante, bears the arms of Pope Julius II. In 1519 Sebastiano de Marforio signed handsome pharmacy vases. After this time many pieces were made. At about 1530 we find the best ware; there were then fifteen potteries at work; at this time Guidobaldo II. called the painter Giambattista Franco from Venice to design for Castel Durante, while Giovanni Teseio and Lucio Gatti carried the art to Corfu, and in 1545 Francesco del Vasaro built a furnace at Venice.

Battisto Franco (born in Venice, 1498, died 1561) studied Michael Angelo's works, and painted the fresco of Minerva Chapel in Rome. He excelled in design, but not in coloring, although Lanzi says his work was in the best style of Florentine art. He engraved metal plates after Raffaele, Giulio Romano, etc., worked entirely with the graver, and marked these B. F. V. F. for Battista Franco Venetus fecit. After 1580 the work declined. In 1623 Pope Urban VIII. altered the name of Castel Durante, his native town, to Urbania. In 1652 the productions were poor, as shown by a vase signed Giambattista Papi; and in the seventeenth century there was a further decline. In 1750 a revival occurred, which copied the conspicuous blue and yellow dresses of the earlier period.

The *candelieri* decoration consists of symmetrical sprays, with scrolls terminating in dolphins, sirens, marine horses, antique masks, and winged monsters, in the favorite style; it is different from the grotesques on white ground seen at Urbino and elsewhere.

The list of Durantine artists is tolerably complete. Among them we find the Peliparii, who changed their name to Fontana; Francesco, an able painter; Francesco del Vasaro, Mo. Diomede Durante, Giovanni Paulo Savino, Giovanni Maria, all of note. Pier del Vasaro, the Sabatini, Picci, Superchina, Savini, Gatti, Bernacchia, Marini, Morelli, worked about 1490, while Francesco di Firenze selected engravings, and Bernardino Dolce gave designs.

The principal artists only painted the central subjects, while the pupils and assistants executed the ornamental borders. The mythological subjects were chiefly executed by Luca, Angiola, and Georgio Picci, Pier Francesco Calze, Ubaldo della Morcia, Simone da Colonello, the Fontanas, the Appoloni, and Lucio, Bernadino, and Ottaviano Dolci. A piece is marked *Giovanni Peruzzi dipinse.*

The revival under the patronage of Cardinal Stoppani developed some well-executed work, which is analogous to the products of Castelli and Naples. Luci and Biscioni are mentioned as producing pottery. The later artists of Urbania, who worked after prints by Sadeler, are Pietro Papi, G. Bertolucci, the Lazzarini, Frattini, and the Biagini; a piece is known marked *Hippolito Rombaldotti, Pinse in Urbania.* To Castel Durante are ascribed certain small cups, with Virgin and Child on yellow ground, in the paste of which dust from the Holy House at Loreto was introduced; they are marked outside, *Con Pol di S. Casa* and *Con Pol et aqua di S. Casa*—that is, "With dust and water of the Holy House."

Characteristics.—The wares from this place are known as Durantine. The clay or body is finer than elsewhere, and of a pale-buff color; the glaze is also richer and more even. An intense dark and rich blue is conspicuous. *Candeliere* decoration is frequently met with, or mixed trophies, grotesques, musical instruments, and Cupids, form the basis of the decorative forms, and the treatment is free, bold, and graceful. *Cerquato* pieces, with yellow oak-branches on a blue ground in compliment to the reigning ducal family of Della Rovere, are frequent; also inscriptions on scrolls. Portrait-plates are a specialty. The carnations are tinted in olive. The coloring is soft. Blue and ochreous yellow are much used for the draperies, and the absence of the brown-red pigment for shading draperies is noticed. A deep, clear brown is also a special color. The painter Francesco Durantino is believed to have painted some of the portrait-plates. Medallions with heads on a yellow ground are frequently seen, and mythological subjects were much in favor.

Piccolpasso, who wrote "The Three Books of the Potter's Art" in 1550, giving a technical history of the art in his time, and also directed a manufactory and designed with skill; and Signor Giuseppe Raffaeli, who, in 1846, published his "Memoirs on the History of the Majolica of Castel Durante," give much information on that subject.

Lead-glazed wares were at first made, and then mezza-majolica; they were coarse, frequently decorated with coats of arms and half-figures, in which the flesh is left white or uncolored.

Various subjects on Castel Durante ware are : Two Cupids, one drawn by the other in a dolphin-car, and holding a child's windmill—S. P. Q. R. on labels at the sides; the shield of arms of Francesco Maria I., supported by two angels—grotesque, with finger-rings set with a pointed stone, a device of the Medici family; bust-portrait of the painter Pietro Perugino; three-quarter face of St. Jerome, with nimbus, and inscription, *Ieronimus ;* a tablet, supported by a cherub's head, inscribed *In nominè dom*, and scrolls, *ama dio ;* cameo-like female head on dark-blue ground, in a wreath with wide oak-branch border (similar borders are placed around shields); Joseph and Potiphar's wife; Neptune and two sea-horses; Hannibal at Cannæ; an equestrian female charging with a spear at a man seated and resting on his shield (above is a Cupid drawn in a car by two doves); portrait of *Cecilia Bella*, within a wreath of green leafage tied by an orange cord; also *Isabeta Beia*; profile-bust of a helmeted warrior, inscribed *Oritia*; portrait of a youth with green cloak and brown hat, inscribed *Capitanio Gintile*; portrait inscribed *Margarita*; *Elena Bella*, with black hat and chain over the neck; *Silvia diva mirabella*, in a dress with yellow sleeves; portrait of Hieronima; *Silvia Bella*, in a yellow dress; a siren holding a shell; a man fishing; a dolphin, the tail terminating in a human mask; drug-vases and albarellos, inscribed *Englosa rodix, Pertarlio odif, in terr Durantis, Mostarda*.

Fig. 8.

f, Dia. Catholicn. M., and ornamented with trophies, dolphins, a turbaned head on a yellow medallion, grotesques of insects, and laureated busts, dated 1556 and 1562; Apollo and Marsyas; rape of Ganymede, 1525.

CASTEL DURANTE.

In Signor Castellani's collection are: The flight into Egypt, 1526; Apollo; arms with *Seigneur nous avons spere en toy;* albarello, with portrait of *Guglielmo edificatore de la Terra de Durante;* Hercules slaying Cerberus, powerfully painted in *camaïeu*, of a dark bluish-green gray, heightened with *bianco fisso* (on the border are six dogs hunting two lions, two bears, and two bulls; the hard firing has caused the enamel to bubble). (See also Figs. 8, 9, and 10.)

CUP ON STAND (Fig. 8).—Coat of arms of the Estensi, guarded by two sphinxes; an open music-book, showing two

FIG. 9.

pages, and inscriptions *Duo* and *Verte folium,* or "Turn the leaf;" musical instruments and grotesques around. The subjects are outlined in gray, tinged with yellowish green, and shaded with the same gray, in a manner called *grisaille*. The notes and the ground are deep blue; ribbon and cross of shield

CASTEL DURANTE. 63

orange-brown; eagles black; scroll of crest and rim yellow. *Bianco fisso* is used on book and grotesques; glaze smooth, brilliant, thick, with some flaws. Castel Durante. Diameter nine and one-half inches. No. 175.

CUP (Fig. 9).—Profile bust-portrait of a young lady, in gray-brown *camaïeu* on yellow-ochre ground, inscribed on ground, *Cintia bela ; bianco fisso* in high lights. Reverse partly enameled, partly unglazed. This piece is executed in a free, broad style. Castel Durante. Diameter four and one-half inches. No. 176.

FIG. 10.

DISH (Fig. 10).—Decorative composition, executed in *grisaille*, of an olive-green gray. There are comic and tragic masks, trophies, expressive heads of horses, arms and armor, shields and greaves, musical instruments, some of a curious shape, a globe, an armillary sphere inscribed (*para*)*diso*, open music-books, one inscribed *bene f*; the letters A. C. on central panel; A. on a side-shield, and a scroll lettered S.P.Q.R.; the whole touched with *bianco fisso*. There are no grotesques, except in the handles of the musical instruments. The play of light and transparent shade is effective, and the piece is undoubtedly beautiful. Castel Durante. Diameter eighteen inches. No. 180.

URBINO.—Passeri remarks that *Urbino* inscribed on pieces does not signify the name of the town, but the patronage of the princes of Urbino, and that the castle of Fermignano contained the works where most of the ware was produced. Most of the artists of Urbino immigrated there from Castel Durante, as is shown by inscriptions such as this: *Historia de Sancta Cecilia, laqualle e fatta in la botega de Guido da Castello Durante, in Urbino*, 1528. The free encouragement extended to artists at Urbino caused the manufacture to flourish as late as about 1630.

In 1477 we find the name of Garducci Giov.; in 1501 that of Francesco Garducci; in 1530 Federigo di Giannantonio, Nicolo di Gabriele, Gianmaria Mariani; in 1542 Simone di Antonio Mariani, Raffaele Ciarla; in 1544 Luca del Fu Bartolomeo. In 1536 Cesare Cari of Faenza painted in the factory of Guido Merlino. In 1535 we find the inscription, *In botega de Mo. Guido Durantino, in Urbino*. In 1542 Guido Merlini or Merligno had a factory at San Paolo; Francesco Xanto worked from 1530 to 1542; Guido Fontana is met with, and is probably the same Guido Durantino who, about 1520, came from Castel Durante and settled in Urbino. His son, Orazio Fontana, produced the best pieces of Urbino ware in a fabrique of his own, 1565. Flaminio, the nephew of Orazio, is known: and Nicola da Urbino. In 1541 we find the fabrique of Francesco de Silvano; in 1585 Gironimo Urbin. The name of Georgio Picchi is met, and that of Francesco Durantino.

Cartoons for majolica plates by Battista Franco, called from Venice in 1540, are known. From 1607 to 1620 several pieces of the Patanazzi family are known.

Characteristics.—The wares of Urbino are usually of a pink or whitish body, and the glaze even; the pieces are left undecorated on the reverse, resembling the Lanfranco wares of Pesaro. The grotesque decoration presents figures more than half-bodied; the scrolls appear to be kept more in abeyance, while the ground is of a purer white, the "bianco di Ferrara" being probably used. The white enamel *sbiancheggiato* is also freely applied over the stanniferous enamel, to give increased brilliancy.

Among the shields of arms are those of the Giorgi or Morosini family, impaled with the Orsini of Rome, of the Salviati, and Della Rovere impaling Montefeltro, with the scroll *Sapies domini situr astris*.

The earlier works of *Francesco Xanto*, Avelli da Rovigo or Rovigiese, were signed in full; the later often have but one or two initials; he also signed in a dozen various ways. His work is very variable in excellence; his drawing is somewhat mechanical, and coloring bright but inharmonious; a vivid black and green are seen; his subjects for *istoriati* are adapted from groups in the compositions of Raphael and other artists, but his subjects are original and show research. Much of his work was subsequently lustred at Gubbio. He had imitators.

Giulio of Urbino affords an instance of an artist who painted at different fabriques, and signed himself as of Urbino, adding the name of the fabrique where he was working.

Guido Fontana has left no signed pieces.

Camillo Fontana is believed to have executed certain pieces defective in the drawing of the figures, particularly of the knees and ankles.

Orazio Fontana, whose father was Guido, who adopted the surname Fontana, and whose grandfather was the potter Nicolo Pellipario of Castel Durante, was the most celebrated of the Urbino artists. He established his works at Urbino in 1565, and died in 1571. The well-known *Spezieria* vases, made for the ducal pharmacy, and now at Loretto, were made at his fabrique. Some of his work is hasty, but much is admirably designed, and shows especially high technical merit. His flesh-tints are first shaded delicately in blue, giving increased atmosphere to the figures. The potting and glazing are also of a high merit. About 1544, pieces with a monogram of Orazio are attributed to him. A service painted by him, after designs by Taddeo Zuccaro, was presented by Guidobaldo to Philip II. of Spain.

Nicola da Urbino is noted for the outlines of his figures, which are finely and carefully drawn, and of Grecian modeling.

Francesco Durantino has left pieces excellent in drawing of outlines and carefully-executed landscapes. Some of his pieces resemble the Urbino ware, and may have been made at Urbino. The flesh is yellow in tone; his horses are drawn with vigor. He also worked elsewhere, as shown by a piece signed *a Mote Bagnolo d' Peroscia*, 1553, probably Bagnara, near Perugia; a plate with a portrait of Raphael is ascribed to him, figured in Delange's *Recueil*.

Among works ascribed to *Nicola da Urbino* are: Standing figure of Venus; the finding of Moses, with an Italian architectural background; Mars, Venus, Vulcan, and Cupids; Camillus freeing Rome from Brennus and the Gauls, with Italian fifteenth-century architectural background, 1543; the chase of the Calydonian boar, 1543. Among pieces ascribed to the *Fontana* fabrique are: two corpses being borne away, inscription "Fa dio stracinar fuor del sacro loco, i corpi di guegli empi scelerati;" Orpheus charming the beasts; Pan and Syrinx, inscribed "Seringa mutata in Cana;" Latona changing into frogs the peasants who insulted her; carriage in a landscape; battle of the Israelites and Amorites; marine deities in the sea, inscribed "Lidi marini;" Cephalus and Procris, inscribed "Come forestier Cefalse a preseta nel 7 d'uvidio 1545;" Pan and Apollo; Vulcan forging arrows for Cupid, and Venus sitting by; Hercules and Dejanira; the story of Myrrha; Perseus and Andromeda; Roman soldiers forcing a landing against armed men; Roman soldiers destroying a bridge—reverse inscription, "Cesar presso a Genana rompe il ponte;" Moses striking the rock, "quando Moise precosse la pietra;" shield of arms surmounted by a prelate's hat; a woman led by Cupid with a leading-string; a plateau painted elaborately on one side with a medallion of Abraham and Melchisedec with grotesque border, on the other a *grisaille* medallion of the Virgin appearing to a traveler; medallions with Bacchanalian subjects in *camaïeu* or one color, surrounded by amusing grotesques; Leda and the swan; Cupid riding on a dolphin; Minerva and the Muses; a sacrifice, ten figures, cattle, camels; Jacob blessing his son; the four apostles; the sons of Jacob plotting against Joseph; Roman lictors in a landscape; wolf (?) holding a heart in his mouth, inscribed "Permerto de mia fe;" the metamorphosis of Apollo; Apollo and Daphne; Venus riding on a dolphin. By *Francesco Xanto* are: Pyramus and Thisbe; a man holding flowers, a female with a lyre, Cupid above with a wreath, 1531; the metamorphosis of Actæon; an adaptation of Raphael's picture of the marriage of Roxana, 1533; Palinurus falling from the galley of Æneas into the sea; the discord of Italy; a turbaned man offers gold carried by a boy to four nude females, and scroll inscribed "Omnia P. pecuniam facta sunt;" Jupiter and Dionysius, the fallen tyrant of Syracuse; the burial of Leucothea; Brutus and Portia. By *Francesco Durantino:* Roman soldiers holding a parley over a stream; Diana and nymphs bathing; incontinence of Calisto; Glaucus and Scylla, 1545. By *Gironimo:* Cupids in *grisaille;* Cupid in a car drawn by two doves; shield bearing a sea-lion. By the *Patanazzi:* Romulus receiving the Sabine women; plateau painted on either side with gods on Olympus, and Minerva and Medusa; panels with a duck in the water, above which is a comet; banquet-scene with Tritons serving. By *various artists:* Gracchus at table, a dragon appearing; Faith holding a cross; Laocoon; Ascanius and Dido; metamorphosis of Daphne; the Holy Family in an interior of the sixteenth century; Apollo and Daphne, inscribed "Dafano mutato in lauro;" rape of the Sabines; the three Graces after Marc Antonio, and on the side a shield surmounted by a cardinal's hat; Phalaris massacred by his subjects; the taking of Alba, with soldiers, cannon, and a castle; a battle-

subject; Venus in the sea standing on a shell drawn by dolphins, Tritons and sea-nymphs at sides, Cupid above; Moses striking the rock, and return of the spies from the promised land; Alexander visiting Diogenes; suppliants before a Roman emperor; a queen on a throne; vine-foliage and grapes; Cupids among blue clouds; Cupids with fruit in a landscape.

In Signor *Castellani's* collection are, besides Figs. 11 and 12: Hercules killing the Hydra, with mark of the fabrique of Guido Durantino, 1535; *Vulcano et Venere;* Cain and Abel; *D'Alcione la vision tremenda e vera*, by Francesco Xanto, 1535; Gyges and Candaules, same painter, 1537; Apollo playing the violin; Narcissus changed to a flower, " Narciso mutato in fiore; " Vulcan forging an arrow; the rape of Proserpine, on the reverse the Pucci arms and *Plutone quando rapi Proserpina;* coronation, *Diquercia coronato Metillino;* woman and Cupid, F. X.; a king addressing his army, attributed to O. Fontana, as also Diana and nymphs, and the massacre of the innocents; a *tazza da partoriente*, with warrior kneeling before a magistrate, and label signifying Francesco Maria, general of the Florentine Republic; two similar tazzas with representations of a woman confined; king speaking to three prisoners; the Holy Family, by *Guido Durantino;* composition of Cupids, Justice, and Chimeras, signed *Christofan de Urb*(ino), a new name, with a companion vase with judgment of Paris and Danaë; judgment of Paris after Marc Antonio, by *Patanazzi;* also the deluge and a cup by the same; Roman aquiliferi and vessilifers; rape of Europa; Pezzo of Urbino, two pieces; Diogenes in his tub; battle, *Cesare abate e sgvizer ala sona;* rape of Europa, attributed to Guido Durantino; and other pieces.

CUP (Fig. 11).—An interesting portrait of Charles V., attributed to Orazio Fontana, resting on a label inscribed: *Progenies. Diem. Quintus. Sic. Carolus. Ille. Imperii. Cæsar. Lumina. et. Ora. Tulit*—Æt. suæ. xxxi.—Ann. M.D.XXXI. On his breast is the lamb of the golden fleece, hanging by a turquoise cord; cap dark indigo blue; velvet corslet dark blue; mantle amaranthine, embroidered; all outlines in olive; flesh shaded in ochre and olive; hair and beard in olive; background around the head bright yellow; left curtain deep purplish blue; right curtain green shaded in olive; the lettering is in blue; yellow rim. *Bianco fisso* is used for the high lights. Urbino. Diameter nine and a half inches. No. 251. Mentioned by Fortnum, p. 337.

FIG. 11.

In connection with Charles V., a lustred plate in Rome signed by Fra Xanto da Rovigo Urbino, 1534, represents a warrior in armor striking with a two-handed sword a nude woman in a somewhat free posture, while five others tremblingly await their fate, and bears the inscription, *Roma lasciva dal buon Carlo quinto partita a Mezza*, or "Rome the wanton, severed in twain by the good Charles V."

TURTLE-BACKED BASIN (Figs. 12, 13, 14, 15, 16, 17).—This piece in the shape of a turtle-shell, serving for a basin or cover, and attributed to Orazio Fontana, is decorated on the underside in imitation of the shell of a turtle, in yellow and black, and with a crab and two shells in high-relief. On the face is a fine illustration of pottery decoration, adapted from Raphael's decoration of interiors. In the centre is a cartouche composed of sirens, amorini, and scrolls, inclosing a military subject. In

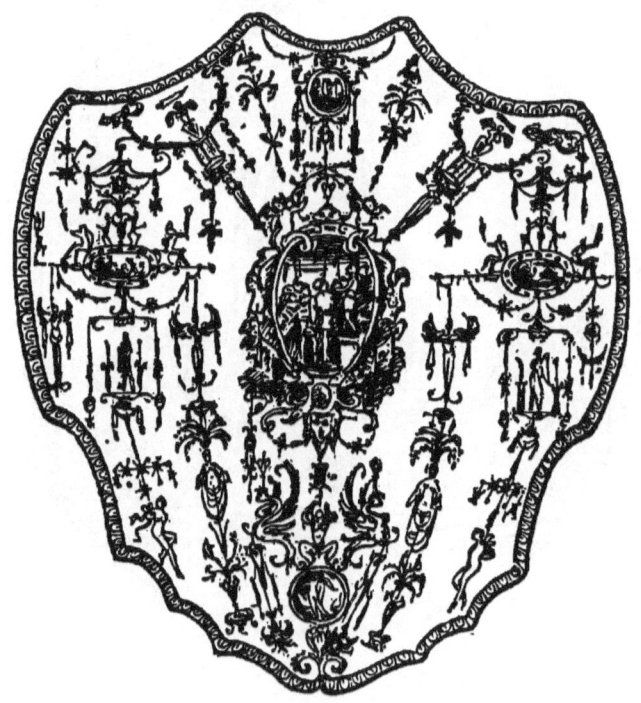

FIG. 12.

the surrounding subjects, which are well distributed and balanced —although not with mechanical precision, from which, however, they lose nothing—are to be seen: *camaïeu* medallions after antique gems, grotesques, masks, rings, coins, arms, birds, baskets of flowers, flaming dishes, festoons, flies, vases, women suspended by one arm, and diminutive imps. The style would rank high, were it not for the expression imparted by the grotesque nudities. The outlines are mostly in olive-green. The drapery is mostly in yellow ochre with blue or brown outline. The wings are blue chiefly, but yellow at the setting on. The flesh is shaded in olive and ochre; the smoke in olive; flame reddish brown. The sprays of small leaves are in black blue. Green is sparingly used, except in the central cartouche. The

FIG. 13.

ground is white; the rim yellow and brown. Urbino. Diameter eighteen inches. No. 275.

GUBBIO.—The first date of 1489 is found upon a lustred piece signed *Don Giorgio*, made probably at Gubbio. The first signed, lustred, and dated piece of Mo. Giorgio is of the year 1519, although a lustred figure, in relief, of St. Sebastian, dated 1501, is fairly ascribable to him. In 1511 he executed two altar-pieces, in the Della Robbia manner, and also one in 1513. He also signed his name in lustre upon many pieces executed by his son, F. Xanto, and others, but to which he applied the lustre enrichment; his last lustred piece is dated 1541.

His son, Vincencio, known also as Mo. Cencio, succeeded to the fabrique, but his signature has not been identified. Later

FIG. 14.

Mo. Perestino worked at Gubbio. He has left pieces marked 1536 *Perestinus*, and 1557 *a di 28 Maggio in Gubbio per Mano di Mastro Prestino*.

The use of lustres at Gubbio was discontinued about 1570. It has been revived in modern days at Gubbio, by Luigi Carocci, of Carocci, Fabbri & Company; by the Marquis Ginori, at the Doccia Works; and by Mr. de Morgan, in England, with some success; also at Fabriano and Pesaro; these modern lustres are, however, still far behind the old in brilliancy, and especially in the beautiful opalescent play of color.

Character.—The lustred wares were chiefly made at Gubbio,

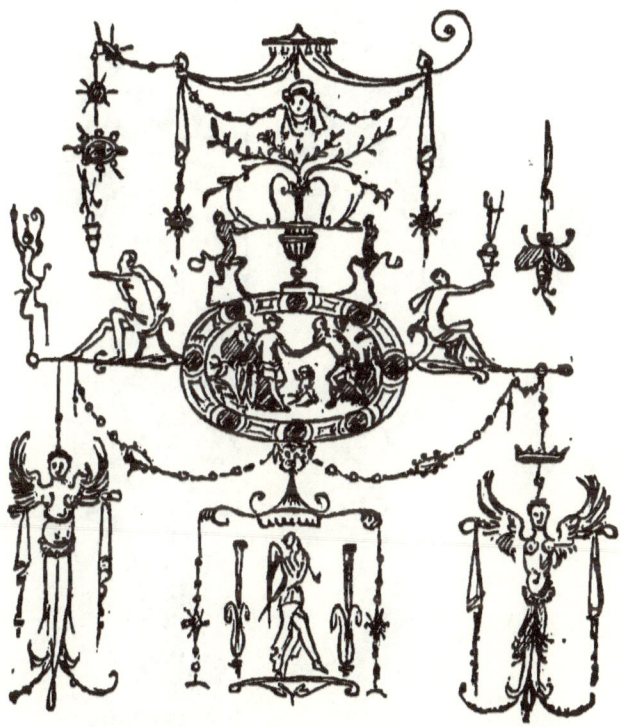

FIG. 15.

but also at Pesaro and Diruta, and perhaps a few pieces at Caffagiolo; so that, when the name of the fabrique or the signature of an artist of Gubbio is not present, other signs besides the lustre must be sought to determine the origin of a piece.

The ornamentation usually consisted of grotesques or foliated scrolls, terminating in eagles, dolphins, human heads, and

4

bodies of animals, together with trophies and masks, resembling, however, in this respect, the Castel Durante designs.

On some pieces from Gubbio the crowned eagle of the Montefeltro house is found; on another, by Mo. Giorgio, the Vitelli arms, dated 1527; on others, those of the Brancaleoni family,

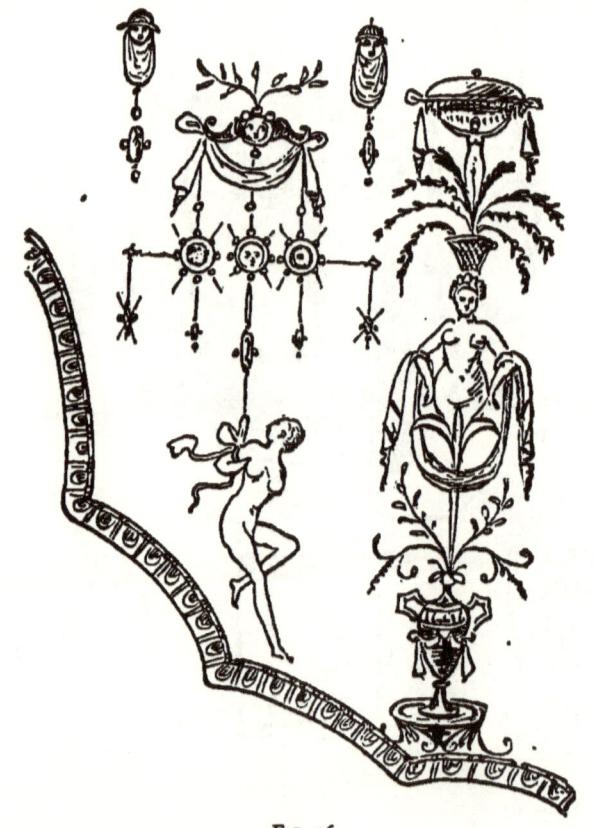

FIG. 16.

of the Duke Francesco Maria I. of Urbino, dated 1521, and of the Martini family of Siena.

NOCERA was a branch of the Gubbio factory; pieces dated 1537, marked with an N, owned by Signor S. Tordelli, are attributed to these works.

GUBBIO. 75

A piece marked *Gualdo*, and heavily lustred in ruby, is variously attributed to Ubaldo, third son of Giorgio, and to an unknown fabrique.

All the illustrations of Gubbio manufacture given below are from Signor Castellani's collection, which is rich in *majolica*. Among the pieces not shown here are some signed by Maestro

FIG. 17.

Giorgio in 1525 and 1528, and twenty-seven others that have been lustred, if not painted, by him. For a list of these and other lustred pieces, amounting to one hundred and thirty-nine in all, the reader is referred to Signor Castellani's catalogue. We will begin with an early piece.

OVAL DISH (Fig.18).—Bust-portraits of two young ladies

in costume of about 1480, or as seen on coins of Lucretia Borgia of 1485. The potting is rude, the form warped, the enamel thick, creamy, and speckled, and partly crackled. The outlines are in blue, and the profiles are relieved by a band of blue; the blue is dark, impure, and presents air-holes, uncovering the buff body. Gold and ruby lustre are applied in ornamental lines and flat tints. The drawing is archaic, free, and rapidly executed. The border, of fruit and leaves, is of early character,

FIG. 18.

somewhat Moresque. A curtain or tent is figured over the heads. Observe the Oriental floral scrolls in background. Gubbio. Three pernetti spots are on the face. Pesaro. Diameters, fifteen and a half and eleven and a half inches. No. 41.

TAZZA DA PARTORIENTE (Fig. 19).—Cupid with hands bound behind his back, with curious, sedate expression. A ruby-lustred ribbon in flying curves enlivens the dark-blue ground, which is also dotted in rows with golden lustre. The border is in rich golden lustre, with slight marbling of ruby. The flesh is creamy, shaded in green. Diameter, six and a half inches. Giorgio Andreoli. No. 47. Excellent in drawing.

Fig. 19.

Istoriati (Fig. 20).—Hercules and Antæus. Reverse, spiral ornament, sun, signature *Maro Giorgia da Ugubio*, 1520, all in yellow lustre. On the face the ruby lustre, which varies from ruby to orange, is applied flat on the hair, lion-skin, and in spare lines on the hair of Antæus and in the trees. The yellow lustre is laid flat upon the club, and in lines on the sandal, hair of Antæus, trees, and sky. The landscape is executed with two shades of blue, two of green, and yellow ochres; rim, yellow. The figures are well drawn. Body light buff; glaze minutely dotted, moderately bright. Three pernetti marks. Diameter, twelve inches. No. 51. Gubbio.

Antæus was son of Poseidon, god of the fluid element, and Ge. He was a mighty wrestler, and invincible so long as he remained in contact with his mother earth. He built a house to Poseidon out of the skulls of all strangers who came to his country, and whom he forced to wrestle with him. Hercules discovered the source of his strength and outgeneraled him by lifting him from the earth and crushing him in air.

This subject is also represented on a salt-cellar of Limoges

Fig. 20.

enamel, made by P. Raymond for Francis I., inscribed *Ercules vincit Antee*.

ISTORIATI (Fig. 21).—Pan and Olympus. A child, carrying a bunch of grapes, pulls the mustache of Pan, seated, holding a red, golden-lustred vase. The figures are outlined in dark-grayish blue, and spirited. The flesh is shaded with blue hatchings, and *bianco fisso* is used for the lights. Hair, bluish green. Ochre, two greens, and dark-bluish gray are used, and a red pigment on vase and stones. Ruby lustre on grapes; golden lustre on horns, vase, grass, clouds, sun-rays. The white-

GUBBIO

Fig. 21.

Fig. 22.

enamel ground varies from a pink to a bluish-white tinge. Reverse floral ornament in yellow lustre. Dated 1528. Gubbio. Maestro Giorgio. Diameter, nine and a half inches. No. 55.

TONDINO (Fig. 22).—Centre, a satyr, with childlike head, holds a snake with one hand and wards it off with the other. Border, a satyr, with melon head-dress, runs off with a lamb, pursued by a horned brother with a stick. Resembles plate shown in Fig. 21, except that ochre as well as blue is used for shading the flesh. The blue is also lighter and less gray. Indigo is used, and *bianco fisso* on flesh, mountains, and sky; landscape, conventional; lustres, ruby and golden; enamel, brilliant, creamy white, finer texture, but still dotted. Mo. Giorgio. Diameter, four inches. No. 57.

FIG. 23.

ISTORIATI (Fig. 23).—Mercury heralding an event. One of the recipients of the news points to another episode, probably the one announced by Mercury, in which ten young women, or men and women, are kneeling before a statue of Minerva, the goddess of war, wisdom, and the liberal arts, mounted upon a large, yellow-lustred vase, and Mercury is flying above.

The outlines are in black-greenish blue; sky, house, landscape, chiefly blue. Mercury has an orange tunic; ruby boots and helmet; wings of helmet gold lustre; caduceus blue. The figure in the doorway has blue dress and light-green mantle. One of the background figures has an orange tunic; another a violet tunic, yellow cloak, ruby boots. The doorway, fort, and

FIG. 24.

statue of Minerva, are in olive *camaïeu*. The flesh is shaded in light ochre and bluish green; the hair is ochreous orange, except Mercury, who has dark-olive hair. *Bianco fisso* is used for the lights. The sky, sun, architecture, and dresses are touched up with lustred lines and ornaments. The drawing is fair, excepting that of the legs. The ruby lustre is deep-red brown, except by reflected light, when it is ruby and violet. The reverse is inscribed 1534, *Mo. Go.*, and with a scroll, in yellow lustre. Mo. Giorgio. Gubbio. Diameter ten inches. No. 59.

TONDINO (Fig. 24). St. Ubaldo, protector of Gubbio. The drawing is archaic; blue outlines, blue shading to flesh; cloak and crozier lemon-yellow. Border outlined in blue, with peculiar apple and short scroll ornaments, found on other pieces; also palmettes. Apples, yellow. The gold lustre varies to violet; the ruby lustre changes from violet to ruby orange. The body and creamy enamel resemble No. 23. Probably about 1520. No other colors are used. The reverse is marked as shown, and with scales, in gold lustre. Mo. Giorgio. Diameter ten inches. No. 62. (Fortnum, p. 194.)

CUP (Fig. 25).—Profile bust-portrait of *Cana Ora Bella*. Out-

FIG. 25.

lined in gray-greenish blue; flesh softly shaded in ochre; eye blue; hair deep-yellow ochre, shaded with lines in ruby lustre, and in part covered with dots of yellow lustre, and a net with blue ornaments; lips yellow. Necklace of ruby-lustre dots, partly burnt off. Dress of a peculiar pink-orange hue, shaded in yellow lustre, with blue scroll ornament. Three chains, a necklace, and ear-rings, in gold lustre over the glaze. Chemise shaded with blue and yellow, and with yellow-lustre pattern, which turns to violet in certain lights. Ribbon shaded in light blue, over which yellow lustre is laid in strokes, which turn the blue to greenish brown. Letters blue, overlaid with gold lustre. Ground dark blue in visible touches, and overlaid with yellow-lustre stars. One touch of *bianco fisso* in the eye. A most harmonious piece. On the underside four G's and the mark shown with date. (See Fortnum, p. 205.) Maestro Giorgio. Gubbio. Diameter nine inches. No. 75.

ISTORIATI (Fig. 26).—Jupiter and Danaë. The flesh is

FIG. 26.

shaded in green and ochre. Ruby lustre on roofs, mantle of Jupiter, flaming rays, shading of rocks and hills. The ruin and the sky surrounding Jupiter are in deep orange, overlaid with golden lustre. The gold lustre is also laid in dashes in the sky, sun-rays, and landscape. The clouds are in olive. Outlines in blue tinged with black. Stanniferous enamel very thick. *Bianco fisso* for high lights. The painting is complex and less harmonious than some simpler pieces. On reverse date 1540, and four G's similar to the one shown. Maestro Giorgio. Gubbio. Diameter ten and one-half inches. No. 76.

DEEP DISH (Fig. 27).—Bust-portrait of a young lady, with

FIG. 27.

scroll inscribed *Camilla B.*, 1541. On the reverse, three G's in ruby lustre. Outlines in blue. Border of arabesques shaded in yellow and lustre on a blue ground. Centre-ground of gold lustre; brilliant. Ruby-lustred head-dress and necklace. Dress striped in gold and ruby lustre. Scroll and flesh shaded in greenish olive and yellow; lips in gold lustre; eyes blue. Gubbio. Diameter fourteen inches. No. 79. Only a portion of the border is shown.

SCODELLA AMATORIA (Fig. 28).—Two hands clasped, with a titular crown above, and border of apples and scrolls in yellow on a blue ground. The subject is traced in firm blue out-

FIG. 28.

line and shaded in blue only; no other color is used. A yellow-lustre pigment is applied on the scale-work of the sleeves, crown, flowers, rim, fruit, and leaves. The lustre is brassy in a direct light, but in reflected light presents nacreous hues of great richness. The enamel is somewhat whiter and less creamy than many pieces. Pesaro? Gubbio? The blue is not pure, but mixed with gray. Diameter nine inches. No. 85.

DISH (Fig. 29).—Profile helmeted bust of a heroine, with

scroll inscribed *Oratio Po*, or *P*. Signor Castellani suggests that this may be the signature of Orazio Pompei, from Castel Durante, who founded a factory in Abruzzo in the early part of the sixteenth century. Traced firmly and boldly in blue, with faint blue shading. A broad blue shade follows the contours on the outside, where shown; the ground is creamy white. A lustre of a somewhat orange color in a direct light, and brassy

FIG. 29.

in reflected light, is applied in many places. The style is admirable. Pesaro? Gubbio? Diameter, twelve and a half inches. No. 87. Only a portion of the border is here shown.

RELIGIOUS CUP, ON STAND (Fig. 30).—A heart in low-relief, pierced by a spear and nails. Above are two weeping eyes, below flames, also in low-relief; border, with oval panels, in relief, and apple ornaments; reverse four G's (Giorgino). The outlines are freely traced in purplish blue; the ornaments are not made with mechanical precision. A brownish-yellow lustre is applied flat on the ovals, leaves, rim, heart, tears, spear, nails, and in scrolls on reverse; the reflections are faint violet and green. A brownish-ruby lustre is laid on the flames, shaft

FIG. 30.

of spear and nails, and apples of border. The enamel is cream-colored and greenish, especially on the reverse. Gubbio. Diameter, nine inches. No. 96. A piece almost similar is dated 1531. This piece has also been considered a *coppa amatoria*.

COPPA AMATORIA (Fig. 31).—Cupid blindfolded, with arms behind his back; Italian landscape background; border, embossed ovals and repeated monogram M. The outlines are in bright blue. The bottom centre is also embossed, and the Cupid is in low-relief, not shaded. Green and ochre are also used. A greenish *madreperla* lustre is laid flat upon the oval panels, rim, trees, quiver, wings, handle of torch, aqueduct, and castle; it varies from green to violet. Where it crosses a blue ground it appears as a bluish-green lustre. A ruby lustre is laid over the round panels, trunk of tree, arrows, bandage, torch-

FIG. 31.

flame, part of castle, and in dots around the neck and on the flying cord. The white-enamel ground is creamy, with fine specks and minute fissures on the reverse. Gubbio. Diameter, nine and a half inches. No. 100.

DISH (Fig. 32).—Profile, half-length portrait of a young lady in sixteenth-century costume, with scroll inscribed *Faustina Pulita e Beia*, or "Faustina, pure and beautiful," and surrounded by a border of cornucopia, jewelry locket, fruit, scrolls, and cartouches bearing TIMOR—DOMINI, or "Fear God." Blue only is used, of a black tinge; outlines delicate, firm, and free. The flesh is faintly shaded in blue, but mainly left white, coming out in striking contrast with the rest of the dish, which has either a blue ground, or is painted in a yellow lustre of nacreous brilliancy, varying from pink and yellow to a superb blue and violet. In certain lights the reflections resemble pol-

FIG. 32.

ished brass. The blue ground shows each brush-mark. Apples are seen in the border. There are two holes in the rim for suspension. The apparent white is probably *terra di Vicenza*. Pesaro or Gubbio? Diameter, sixteen and a half inches. No. 161.

TWO-HANDLED VASE ON STAND (Fig. 33).—On each side a deer reposing in the sun. Decoration in Persian character, of trees and foliage. The outlines are in blackish blue, archaic, and a yellow color is laid flat in the ornamental forms and on the handles. This yellow is everywhere overlaid with a nacreous lustre (except on one yellow, unlustred handle), which changes from yellow through green to violet and ruby. The

FIG. 33.

even distribution produces at first the impression that the entire surface is lustred. The white enamel is brownish creamy, with many fine cracks. The ornament is similar to that on Fig. 24. Pesaro? Gubbio? Height, eight and a half inches. No. 168.

BASIN (Fig. 34).—In the centre a hare bounding. Perspective ground, not in accordance with the position of the floral ornaments. Radiating border, in which a certain balance is obtained by opposite radiations in the outside rim; the running action of the hare is repeated in the border, which appears to whirl. The blue outlines are relieved by an accompanying band of blue. The hare and flowers are yellow; a silvery lustre is lavishly applied. An effective piece. Pesaro or Gubbio. Diameter, thirteen inches. No. 171e.

FIG. 34.

In other collections, pieces attributed to Mo. Giorgio represent: *Pulisena B* and heart transfixed; rabbit on a rock; female bust, *Baldasina;* Cupid riding a unicorn; two of St. Francis receiving the stigmata, 1518 and 1532; Cupid nursing a dog; a leopard and a lion holding a tree; Virgin and Child; three horsemen fighting for a standard, three others wounded; death of Pyramus; Diana and Actæon; man and woman embracing by the stream of life; woman at a well, 1525; Tritons and seanymphs; a saint between two dogs, and letters S L; a man felling a tree which is turning into a nymph, a man looking on, a corpse and severed head on the ground. Interesting lustred pieces by other artists are: Cupid holding a fox by the tail, 1525; *Daniella Diva* and burning heart inscribed *oime* between two doves, 1530; Romulus and Remus suckled by the wolf; female portrait, *Amaro chi me amara;* Angelica bound to a rock delivered from the monster by Ruggiero, who is mounted on a hippogriffin, 1549, inscribed *Angellica ligata al duro scoglio*, from the story in Ariosto; portrait of *Julia Bella*.

CITTA DI CASTELLO, near Gubbio, is mentioned by Piccolpasso as producing *graffio* pieces by a method which he calls *à la Castellana*, in which a white slip of *earth of Vicentia* is laid on the colored unbaked ware; a low heat is then applied; the surface is next scratched or engraved; a much thinner slip of the same white earth is again applied, and the object is then well fired. A yellowish lead-glaze, a bright yellow, copper-green, in faint, clouded patches, and touches of black and blue, are also applied upon the white slip. At Foligno and in Lombardy similar *sgraffiati* were produced, and the process is seen upon plates of the twelfth and thirteenth centuries incrusted in churches.

BAGNOLO.—A piece by Francesco Duranno (1533) bears this name.

THE MARCHES.

FAENZA.—This place has disputed with *Faiance*, near the Pyrenees in France, the honor of originating the term *fayence* for all descriptions of glazed earthenware. Although in about A. D. 590 crockery is known to have been made at Faiance, nothing shows that it was otherwise than plain, and it seems probable that the beauty of the Faenza wares, which were early imported in vessels into France, attracted attention, and originated the application of that name to earthenware.

In 1485 Garzoni mentions the distinguishing whiteness and polished glaze of the earthenware of Faenza. In the beginning of the sixteenth century the designs increased in perfection.

Baldasára Manara, of Faenza, 1536; Nicolo da Fano, 1521;

Giov. Brama, of Palermo, 1546; Petrus Andre de Fave; Giuliano Gambyn; Domenico Tardessir, 1574; and Cesare Cari—were Faentine artists. Drug-pots, marked *Andrea Pantaleo pingit*, 1616, are known. Vergilio, Mo. Francesco, Francesco Vicchij (1639), directed fabriques at Faenza; and the Casa Pirota fabrique of that place is well known in 1525 and 1530.

The seventeenth-century wares are rarely seen. A modern fabrique, the Farina Artistic Ceramic Company, at Faenza, produces ware in the style of the old, but usually inferior. Some good artistic plaques, however, are shown. A peculiar black and dark green are much used there. The lustre is coarse.

Characteristics.—The whiteness and polish of the fifteenth-century ware are known. *Sopra-bianco* ornament, or white on pale-pink ground, is met with. A timid, weak style of drawing, but executed with particular technical skill, is a feature; and a pear-shaped mask, with beard spreading into acanthus-leaves, is a favorite. In pieces of the Casa Pirota fabrique the drawing is good, however.

The Casa Pirota mark, of a crossed circle, with or without a crescent, is usually found on pieces with wide borders, decorated with grotesques left white, and shaded in yellow and pale-blue ground, called *a berettino*, or reserved in gray heightened with white on a dark-blue ground, known as *sopra azurro*. In some cases the blue has been mixed with the glaze. *Bianco sopra smaltino*, or white on a gray ground, is also used.

A red pigment called *rosso di Faenza* is used here as well as at Caffagiolo; and both places use concentric lines of blue, yellow, and orange, on the reverse and spirals. *Smartellato* or *Scannellato* pieces made in fluted ornamented moulds are frequent; also perforated work. The later *istoriati* pieces have usually no mark, or only concentric lines. Pieces in the style of those in the Correr Museum, with thin, liquid colors, and of much artistic merit, are attributed to Faenza.

The arms of Bologna, with her motto, *Libetas ;* the keys of St. Peter; the arms of the Manfredi, of the Lando families, of Strozzi impaling Ridolfi, of Strozzi impaling Medici, are found;

and the name is written either Faventcie, Faenza, Fave, or Faenca, indifferently.

Among pieces bearing the Casa Pirota mark, or ascribed to it, are: The sacred monogram I. H. S.; Curtius leaping into the gulf; a crest, surrounded by border of Cupids playing, *sopra azurro*, and a rim of grotesques, is very effective; shield of arms surmounted by a cherub's head; Cupid bearing a shield of arms; the adoration of the shepherds; Christ and the woman of Samaria; Christ bearing his cross, after the painting by Raffaele known as Lo Spasimo di Sicilia; Mutius Scævola; half-figure of Moses; imitation of Venetian enameled dish. Among the *Scannellati*, or moulded pieces, are: A figure of a saint; the Magdalene kneeling in a glory; a saint seated on a cloud; man in Eastern dress; a Cupid; portrait inscribed *Flamino;* St. Sebastian; Cupid with a vase; Judith with the head of Holofernes; a woman holding a pierced heart; Justice. Among other pieces of Faenza are: Joseph sold by his brethren; the judgment of Solomon, inscribed *Non mi chi nec tibi sed dundiatur;* the Resurrection; Hercules with the distaff and Omphale, Cupid at her feet, and motto, *Omnia vincit amor*, 1522; the gathering of the manna, from an engraving by Agostino Veneziano, after Raffaele; the adoration of the Magi; a sleeping knight, and a man in civil dress, with winged cap, holding a globe; St. George and the dragon; the *Veronica*, or napkin, bearing the impress of the countenance of our Saviour; Cupids riding dragons, and Cupid holding a skull; hands joined; many drug-pots, one with the head of an old man, inscribed *Justinian Imp.;* another, with an old man, in yellow coat and hood, kissing a richly-attired lady, inscribed *A. Capillor. ne.*

PLATE (Fig. 35).—Central yellow coat of arms on a blue ground, and bearing a scorpion. The shield is surmounted by a helmet and scrolls, and upheld by two boys in gray *camaïeu*, with *bianco-fisso* light. The rim is yellow, and a green, vine-like border next to it. The chief surface of the border presents a faint, gray ground, with superposed *bianco-fisso* ornaments, as shown in black on the sketch instead of white. The reverse bears the date 1544. The effect is delicate and rich. Faenza. Diameter eighteen inches. No. 212 of Signor Castellani's collection, in which are also the following subjects from Faenza and Romagna: The Virgin St. Roque and St. Sebastian; Apollo and Daphne; *Gabriella. Be. Lodivieta;* a woman whipping an old man, *Antini. annas. pare. al. sz. cet.;* Judith holding the head of

FIG. 35.

Holofernes; St. James the Less; various coats of arms, surrounded by sea-monsters, Cupids on hippocampi, a seraph with string of pearls, trophies; Apollo combating Martias, and Apollo skinning Martias; old man reading a book, *Ebreo* written above; *Otavio* bust; Fortitude; Diana; St. Jerome; bust of a Sibyl before an open book; child holding a basket of fruit; bust of a cardinal before an open book; figure in devotion; arms, *Sordileta. di. Navare.* MDXXXV; arms, *Va.*

integro; Alexander before Diogenes, who rests under a tree (warrior, falconer, dogs, servants, pages, and coat of arms, are also on the piece, and date 1524); troubadour playing on flute; Cupid playing violin; Satyr; pine-shaped vase; flask, St. Roque; warrior leading a woman to a field of briers, *A. Apiit;* and other pieces.

BOCCALETTO (Figs. 36 and 37).—These small pitchers, respectively six and five inches high, are of early appearance.

FIG. 36.   FIG. 37.

The interior of the first is glazed with lead, and the exterior faintly glazed, and of grayish paste. The letter A is outlined in manganese, and filled in with green. The second has no interior glaze, but a faint, thin exterior glaze applied over a clay slip of lighter color than the body. The ornaments, outlined in manganese, with some copper-green in flat tints, resemble those on known early Italian pieces, and appear to be a rude copy of Oriental patterns. The ornament on the farther side of 37 is figured next to it. Romagna. Nos. 192 and 193.

OVOID VASE, WITH TWISTED HANDLES (Fig. 38).—On one side the coat of arms of the Orsini family shown on a smaller scale.

On the other, within a border, a label inscribed in Gothic letters, as shown, which may be read: *Non ti ralegrare del mio duolo, excelpelto quando el mio sera voto*, or, "Do not rejoice at my pain, excepting when I am empty." The chief color is blue, pur-

FIG. 38.

plish used for outlines, lettering, handles, etc. A rich orange is also used. The white-enamel ground is thin and flowing, but crackled all over. Romagna. Height eleven inches. No. 199. The analogy between this early shape and the Persian is seen.

FORLI.—In 1396 the potter Pedrinus Joannis is cited as emigrating to Pesaro. In the sixteenth century Forli possessed an important fabrique. A piece dated 1542, *fata in Forli;* also Maestro Iero, Jacomo from Ripa Grande, 1593; Leucadio Sombrino, of Forli, 1555—are known.

Characteristics.—Some of the wares resemble technically those of Caffagiolo; others imitate the Faenza style and mark of the Casa Pirota, but add *Fata in Forli ;* but they are inferior to Faenza.

Painted tiles, with inscriptions and portraits, are met with. "The Massacre of the Innocents," after Baccio Bandinelli, boldly drawn, and other pieces, showing breadth and harmonious color, prove that Forli had some good artists. Maestro Iero painted in a bold and able manner. The *porcellana* style, of light blue on white, reminding one of Oriental porcelain, is found here as well as at Siena, Ravenna, and Fabriano. Examples of subjects from Forli are: The Virgin and Child; boys gathering fruit from a tree, and arms of Matthias Corvinus; two shields of arms surmounted by a crown, those of Matthias Corvinus, King of Hungary; profile portrait, with grotesque border; a cartouche inscribed *Giacinta B.;* a winged woman, with a sceptre in her right hand, and a broken column under her left, inscribed *Forteza ;* floral scale, diapered border; Santa Veronica holding the vernicle; Christ disputing with the doctors, border of musical instruments; portrait of *Camilla* on a raised shield; tiles, with portraits and long inscriptions, from a villa at Pieve-a-Quinto, dated 1513. Among the portraits are: *Niron, Chamilo, Sase, Charlomn, Stephanus Nardinus,* the doge *Cechus de Rubeis,* with the addition, *Principus que Venecia ; Ugolinus Music,* a celebrated composer; *Melotius Pitor, Carolina,* and *Leta ;* vase with palmette ornament; children holding alternately a shield and a mandolin; a boar among cypress-trees; on a raised centre-shield the initials P P, surrounded by four medallions, containing profile portraits of ladies, and knights in armor; wide belts of white palmette ornament outlined in blue, on orange ground; a wide belt with medallions, with helmeted and turbaned heads and a figure of Justice, inscribed *Justitia dedio ;* a rude figure severing the head of a vanquished warrior; shield of arms surmounted by a mitre.

RIMINI.—Pieces dated 1535 in Rimini, and others marked *Rimini,* have come down to us. They are characterized by the noted brilliancy of their glaze—pale flesh-tints shaded with ochreous hatchings, black tinge of the blue, and generally dark tone of shading. The subjects are Biblical and mythological. The reverse is sometimes marked with concentric yellow lines.

IMOLA has been referred to as producing white enameled terra-cotta.

RAVENNA.—A plate ably painted in blue *camaïeu* on gray-blue ground, marked *Ravena* on the reverse, has been brought to light by Baron Davillier.

BOLOGNA is referred to by Piccolpasso, but no Bolognese work has reached us earlier than 1870, when good copies of Della Robbia's work were produced there.

STATES OF THE CHURCH.

DERUTA.—In 1461 Agostino di Antonio di Duccio, pupil of Luca della Robbia, went to Perugia, and there executed a frieze for the church of S. Bernardino in enameled terra-cotta; and is supposed to have influenced the Deruta school, at which neighboring town we find lustred pieces, as shown by the earliest dated piece (1535), *fatta in Deruta*, decorated in gold lustre on a blue ground, in M. Fountaine's collection; and lustred pieces in low relief are by some attributed to Diruta. The mark upon a lustred piece, *El Frate in Deruta pt.*, 1541, gives the key to a number of pieces signed *El Frata*, from 1541 to 1545. Made in Deruta by a monk or an order of monks, they are recognized by their brassy, golden lustre, dull enamel, and loose, inaccurate drawing, traced in brown or blue. On a lustred plate, representing Phœbus pursuing Daphne, is the mark *Febo Dafene in Deruta*, 1544, with a P. A lustred piece—subject, Alexander and Roxana—is inscribed *Deruta fe el Frate pemise.*

Among lustred pieces *attributed* to Deruta, on account of the brassy hue of the lustre, are a profile helmeted head, after G. B. del Porto; a plate—subject, Diana and Actæon—both superior in drawing; a fine dish, with Santa Cecilia after Raffaele. In later days an inscription shows that Gregorio Caselli had a fabriqué of lustred *majolica fina* at Deruta in 1771.

Unlustred pieces are also known. The inscriptions *Francesco Urbini i Deruta*, 1537; *i Deruta il Frate pensi*, 1545; 1545, *in Deruta Frate fecit;* the letter D with a paraph—are met with.

Characteristics.—The general style may be said to be an inferior copy of Pesaro and Gubbio, with a certain breadth, however, and absence of details; and the lustre is partly golden, partly brassy, with occasional pearly reflections. The enamel ground is coarse, opaque, and creamy in color, and the blue is deep and dull. The flesh is usually shaded in blue. The ruby lustre is absent, or present only as a pale, faint lustre. The work of the brotherhood of monks is heavy and rude in drawing, and quite inferior where several colors are used. Occasionally a Persian ornament is found on the reverse. It is not unlikely, however, that another fabrique existed at Deruta, in which relief-pieces and superior work were executed.

Where the name Antonio Lafreri is met among works, it merely shows that his work was copied, as he is known as a sixteenth-century engraver at Rome.

Among lustred pieces of Deruta, in various collections, are the following subjects: Profile-bust of woman, inscribed *Sura fiore;* Liberty holding a heart and a cornucopia, inscribed *Non bene pro toto libertas venditur auro finis;* cartouche, with the word *Ave;* Cupid frightened at a skull; Hercules and Nemean lion; Sol in his chariot; a man washing the head of an ass seated in a chair, inscribed *Chi lava il capo a l'asino, Se perd. o.* 1556.

The unlustred pieces ascribed to Deruta present various subjects, among which are: a Cupid shooting, standing on a platform drawn by dolphins, ridden by cherubs, other Cupids blowing trumpets behind; the Virgin seated between a floating angel holding a lily, while another holds an olive-branch; blindfolded Cupid shooting; portrait of *Lorenza Bella; De Pluton e Proserpine in disparte,* 1546; a label bearing the word *Chamilla;* Cupid, holding a pennon, riding a galloping horse; a dance of Cupids after Marc Antonio; Actæon changed to a stag, *Il miser Ateon conuerso i ceruo;* two lovers under a tree, Cupid hovering above, ships in background; Juno praying Æolus to send contrary winds against Æneas; a device of three hillocks surmounted by flames, and surrounded by a wreath of fruit.

FABRIANO has left several pieces, notably one marked *Fabriano*, 1527; a copy of an engraving, by Marc Antonio, of Raphael's "Madonna della Scala," executed with breadth and ability. In modern days, Cesare Miliani & Co. produce cleverly-lustred pieces there; the copper lustre is good, ruby fair, and a brassy lustre with violet reflections promises well.

FOLIGNO.—Piccolpasso gives the drawing of a water-mill, used to grind colors at Foligno, and states that these colors were used on a slip of white Vicenza clay, in the method called *alla Castellana*.

SPELLO, in the Marches of Ancona, produced a fine, light-colored potter's earth, in the time of Piccolpasso.

VITERBO.—On the face of an interesting, rudely-decorated piece, in the Kensington Museum, is a scroll inscribed *In Viterbo Diomeo*, 1544.

ROME.—On the fall of the duchy of Urbino, M. Diomede, from Castel Durante, established a fabrique at Rome. The inscriptions *Fatto in botega de M. Diomede Durante in Roma*, and on a companion-piece, *Fatto in Roma da Gio. Paulo Sabino, MDC*, and *Alma Roma*, 1623, are met with. The style of these wares, of about 1600, is that of the Urbino grotesques.

Later, in 1790, Giovanni Volpato, an engraver of Venice, made figures of biscuit porcelain in Rome; he next manufactured glazed earthenware, saints, and bust-portraits, and some admirably-modeled statuettes, marked *G. Volpata, Roma ;* this fabrique ceased in 1831. Signor Torquato Castellani makes to-day excellent unlustred copies of the old fayence, outlined in dark-purplish blue, and painted on the raw enamel before this is fired.

In Signor Alessandro Castellani's collection are a cup inscribed *Roma. Anno. Jubilei*. 1600; a vase, *Roma fecit*, 1620; *boccale* in the style of Gian Paolo Savino; St. Benedict, 1606, Botega of G. P. Savino; coat of arms; Venus and Cupid, with coat of arms and *L. B.*, and other arms with *S. Benedetto*, 1597, also from the same.

SOUTHERN ITALY.

Southern Italy has a separate history. Tradition carries us back to the arrival of Œnotrus from Arcadia, 1710 B. C., and of Evander, 1240 B. C. Lavinium is said to have been founded by a colony of expatriated Trojans, who came with Æneas from Troy, 1182 B. C. The Greek colony of Parthenope, about 1000 B. C., divided its capital into *Paleopolis* (the old city) and Neapolis (the new city), from which Naples. About 326 B. C. the Romans conquered it. Next came Theodoric the Ostrogoth, 493 A. D. Belisarius took possession for the Oriental Empire, 536 A. D.; Totila in 543. Retaken by Narses for Byzantium in 552 A. D., and invaded by the Saracens in the ninth century. In 1131 Roger the Norman founds the kingdom of the Two Sicilies. The German house of Hohenstaufen next rules Naples, 1194 to 1266. Then Charles of Anjou holds it for France, until, in 1435, Alfonso V., of Aragon, seizes Naples; Charles VIII., of France, takes it in 1494; but in 1504 Naples and Sicily are united to Spain; an extortionate rule leads to Massaniello's revolt in 1647. In 1706 Eugene of Savoy conquers Naples. In 1714 the Treaty of Utrecht gives Naples to Austria. In 1735 the Treaty of Vienna gives it to the Bourbons of Spain. Naples next forms a short-lived republic, then a kingdom, which Murat holds, till, in 1815, the allies restore it to the Bourbons.

In Calabria is found a colony of Albanians, who came there from Epirus in 1532 A. D., and have remained separate, and of the Greek religion, to this day.

NAPLES.—In the sixteenth and seventeenth centuries Naples produced large fayence, caryatide-handled vases handsomely decorated, on one face in blue *camateu* touched with black, with religious subjects. On one is written *Franco Brand. Napoli Gesu novo ;* on another, *Paulus Francus Brandi Pinx* 68; and, again, *P. il sig. Francho Nepita,* 1532, and marked with a five-pointed crown, which is closed on the top, differing thus from the Bassano crown.

At the fabrique of *Capo di Monte,* established 1736 by Charles

III., a well-known fine porcelain and some fayence-pieces were made, marked *Capo di Monte Molo*.

At this day Giustiniani, Mollica, and others, produce fayence and terra-cotta, of a hard, pale-buff body, with the name stamped in the paste, coated with a thick, flowing enamel, and of variable artistic merit.

GROTAGLIA, near Tarento, produced dishes marked with the arms of the Martina family.

CASTELLI, distinguished as Castelli in Abruzzo, produced in the fifteenth and sixteenth centuries pottery as celebrated as that of Pisa and Pesaro, as testified to by Antonio Beuter in 1540; its early character is not known, but the names of *Nardo di Castelli* (1484), *Antonius Lollus a Castellis inventor, Orazio Pompei* (1551-'88), and *O. Pompei the younger* (1610), have come to us in connection with paintings on pottery. In the seventeenth and eighteenth centuries the work of the families of Grue, Gentili, Capelleti, and Fuina, is celebrated; the drawing is correct and free, a characteristic paleness pervades the colors, which are tasteful and harmonious, and gilding is occasionally applied; the subjects are chiefly Biblical.

Of the Grue family are known—Francesco (1647), Fs. A. Grue Espeprai (1677), Dr. Franc Antonio Caver Gru (1718), Fras. Anto. Grue (1722-'38), F. A. Saverio Grue (1749). Carl Antonio Grue, who signs C. A. G., is thought the best painter. His son, Liboricus Grue, signs L. G. P.

Bernardino Gentile (1670), Luc. Anto. Ciannico (1733), Math Roselli, G. Rocco di Castelli (1732), and Carlo Coccorse, have signed as painters. Signor A. Castellani owns three portrait-pieces, one of Tomaso Aniello, Greco d'Amalfi, his father, and Bernardina Pisa, Massaniello's wife.

'In Signor Castellani's collection are a piece by Gesualdo Fuina, eighteenth century; Venus and Anchises, by Carmine Gentile; also two pieces, *Liborio Grue pinxit;* and eight by Carlo Antonio Grue, representing Summer, Justice, Orpheus and Eurydice, landscapes, etc.; and the following:

PLATE (Fig. 39).—This piece is a fair example of the Castelli manufactures. In the centre an allegorical figure, holding a lamb, and a child at her feet holding a label marked MAN-SVETVDO. The subject is *Meekness*.

FIG. 39.

The body is buff, coated with a pure white, somewhat bluish enamel. The figures are outlined with a soft, reddish-brown ochre. Flesh lightly tinted in yellow ochre, and shaded in same with blue hatchings. Leaves and shadows of lady's robe are dark green, the robe itself yellow. Chemise white, shaded in blue; curtain, brown; flowers, both blue, white, and yellow ochre; Cupids' drapery, two blue, two green; masks, in yellow and ochre. The background of the border is a rich, dotted yellow. There is abundant gilding in little dabs on all the drapery, and on other portions. Carlo Antonio Grue. Diameter, seven and a half inches. No. 309.

PALERMO AND CATALA GIRONE.—We have separated the

lustred Siculo-Arabian ware of an earlier date from those of the sixteenth century. Near the ruins of ancient ovens at Catala Girone these wares were found mixed in fragments of all periods. M. Davillier owns an albarello inscribed *Fatto in Palerma*, 1606, partly resembling in decoration the Castel Durante.

GRAFFITI

is the name given in Italy to earthenware ornamented by means of " scratching," from *graffiare*, to scratch. They are sometimes called *sgraffiti*, from *sgraffiare*, which has the same meaning. Piccolpasso describes the process as practised at Città di Castello.

A white earth, or *terra di Vicenza* (probably a marl, or limy clay), is ground in water and laid on the unbaked red clay body; the object is then lightly fired, to obtain a determined degree of adhesion of the white "slip;" the drawing is then traced or scratched upon this surface with an iron point, so as to let the darker body underneath appear in the lines of the drawing. The piece is then dipped in a transparent glaze, and fired again. In addition to this process, the subject was sometimes painted in colors upon the white earthy ground, which contained no tin, and the pieces were then called *alla Castellana*.

The dates attributed to the *graffiti* are about from 1300 to 1700. In the South Kensington Museum Catalogue will be found a description of sixteen pieces. One shows a mandolin-player, and two figures in fifteenth-century costume. One, by *A. M. Curtius*, of Pavia, is dated 1694. In other collections are pieces dated 1525 and 1624. M. Jacquemart figures a French plate inscribed *Je cuis planter pour raverdir. Vive Truppet*, and a cup with raised and incised mouldings, engraved with a mandolin-player between a lady singing and one playing on the tambourine, in costumes of the second half of the fifteenth century.

The *sgraffio* process is used occasionally on handsome pieces of modern earthenware.

PERSIA.

THE space given to the following historic details will be thought justified, it is hoped, by the interest which attaches to the origin of objects that surround us.

With the exception of the Greeks—and perhaps they should not be excepted—no ancient race has stamped its taste and feelings upon subsequent times with the distinctness and force of the Persians. A few illustrations displaying the Persian type are given in these pages, and it may be regretted that so few examples of excellence are accessible; although the more common types, modified but not often improved upon by others, are well known. Those who are less acquainted with the original style will perhaps follow with some interest the attempt to indicate, in a brief manner, some of the obscure ways by which these types have reached us, and are still living forms of decoration familiar to us in metallic ware, pottery, chintzes, damasks, carpets, wall-papers, and architectural forms.

The language of the first Persian Empire belongs to the Indo-European family, which has been traced (with the movements of the Aryan race) from the Bactrian Zend through the Vedic, Sanskrit, Pali, Pakrat, etc., in the East, and in the Greek, Latin, and Teutonic languages in the West. Their ancient kings, however, as shown by the monumental cuneiform inscriptions, published their edicts in each of the three great branches of human language, as they do to-day, in Persian, Turkish, and Arabic.

An indication of Persian influence upon India is seen in the court language of Delhi, which is Persian, as also that of the more polished Mohammedans throughout India.

History.—The first Persian Empire, founded by Cyrus 558 B. C., extended westward under his successors to the shores of the Mediterranean, including Egypt, the line of the Black Sea and Caucasus on the north, Bactriana and Sogdiana, the line of the Indus on the east, and the Arabian Sea and Indian Ocean on the south. This vast empire came to a close by the invasion and conquest of Alexander, B. C. 331.

The Greco-Bactrian kingdom lasted about a century, when an irruption of the Scythians overthrew it. The Parthian kingdom, founded by Arsaces 208 B. C., followed, and gradually extended from the Euphrates to the Indus, until, in 226 A. D., the Persian chief Ardesheer (Artaxerxes) overturned the Parthian dynasty, and founded the Sassanian, or second Persian Empire. He also assumed the title of Shah-in-Shah, or King of Kings, and his dynasty reigned over Persia 415 years, until the Arab invasions in 632 A. D. and the few following years.

The religion of Zoroaster prevailed in Persia previous to the conquest by the Arabs, who introduced the Mohammedan religion, which gradually became the prevailing faith. In the seventh century art and industry flourished in Persia. From this time forward, to trace the movement of Persian ideas and methods in their influence on architecture and the industrial arts in Europe is merely to follow the successive invasions and conquests of the Arabs, Saracens, and Moors, in Spain, Byzantium, among the islands and along the shores of Southern Europe. Thus the Arabs and Turks derived their musical instruments and their music from the Persians, while from the Moors in Spain the English derived the gittern (*kuitra*), the lute (*el-oud*), the rebec (*rehab*), the naker (*nakarra*). Also, in textiles, the word *muslin* comes from the city of Mosul; *buckram* from Bokhara; *baldakin*, or baudekin, from Baldak or Bagdad; *ciclatoun*, which means in Persian *bright and shining*, was an early name in Europe for certain glossy silk; *satin* is from *aceytuni*; cloth of *Tars* indicates its origin; *sarcenet* is a thin silk named from its Saracen makers. From Persia, we have the game and name of *chess;* from "shah," king, and, in Moorish, sheik; checkmate is from "shah-mata," *the king is dead;* and the story is told that Tamerlane had just castled a king when the birth of a son was announced to him, whom he accordingly called "Shah Rookh." Persian enameled glass is known; a specimen of the sixth century, enameled on gold, exists in the Public Library at Paris. The early Venetian glass presents Persian patterns. Many other examples might be given. The observations suggested by the movement in different countries and localities will be found in the respective chapters appropriated to each, and the few remarks which follow will be confined to Persia and its more immediate surroundings.

The invasion of Persia by the Arabs under Khaled, in 632 A. D., resulted in the defeat of Isdegerd III., the last Sassanide king, and the establishment of the Mohammedan power, 651 A. D. Four centuries of dissension and anarchy followed, and in 1086 the Persians had sufficiently recovered to take the offensive: they invaded Palestine, seized Jerusalem, spread dismay in Byzantium, which contributed to the uprising in Europe that led to the first Crusade in 1096.

The great movement under Genghis Khan swept over Persia in 1223, and resulted in the establishment of the vast empire of the Moguls, which extended from the Tigris to Peking. The Tartar Tamerlane (1370–1402) revived the decaying power of the Moguls, reconquered Persia, and carried his arms to the shores of the Mediterranean, to Moscow, and to India, where he firmly established his rule.

In 1407 the Turkoman dynasty of Kara-Koin-Lu (*Black Sheep*) appeared in Persia, followed by the dynasty of Ak-Koin-Lu (*White Sheep*) in 1468. The latter were of the Mohammedan sect *Schiah*, followers of Ali, nephew and son-in-law of the Prophet, and, in their opinion, his rightful successor. To this sect the Persian Mohammedans adhere at the present day, and are in sectarian opposition to the *Sunni*, the followers of Abubeker, one of the fathers-in-law of Mohammed, which includes the Turks.

In 1501 Ismael, a Sophi or mystic, and descendant of Ali, founded in Persia the dynasty of Sophis. He was followed by several brief reigns until 1585, when the Shah Abbas seized the throne, restored order, made concessions to the Turks, consolidated his power, embellished his capital Ispahan, recovered his Turkish concessions, and became distinguished for the splendor of his reign and his piety. He was followed by Shah Sophi, 1626, who lost Bagdad to the Turks, and was succeeded, 1642, by Shah Abbas II., who enlarged his dominion on the side of India. Under him Ispahan attained its highest splendor. It was visited at this time by Chardin and Tavernier, whose valuable observations are well known.

Soleiman succeeded to the throne in 1666, and Hussein in 1694-1722. These two reigns were disastrous: internal discord prevailed; the Afghans, having massacred the Persians in India, 1710, laid siege to Ispahan and overturned the government, while the Turks seized the western provinces, and the Russians the northern, 1722. At this date Shah Thamas, the son of Hussein, came into power, and, with his brigand general, Nadir Kouli, expelled the Afghans and Turks, 1729; but, having made humiliating terms with the Turks, 1732, was dethroned by Nadir, who proclaimed Abbas Mirza, the son of Thamas, then one year old, his successor. Nadir then completed the expulsion of the Turks, and restored the ancient limits. Mirza soon died, and Nadir was crowned with great ceremony. He continued his military operations with success, laid the Afghans and Moguls under tribute, annexed the region west of the Indus, sacked Delhi, took Khiva and Bokhara, proclaimed an edict of tolerance in favor of the Sunni, and was assassinated, 1747. Several brief reigns followed, and confusion prevailed until (1795) the advent of Khadjar (Aga Mohammed Shah), the founder of the existing dynasty, who was successful in arms. He was assassinated, 1797, and followed by his nephew, Futteh Ali Shah, who was engaged in wars with Russia, Turkey, and the Afghans. The dissensions of the Sunni and Schiahs subsided before the dangers which arose from the attitude of Russia and England; Persia, however, maintained the autonomy of her empire, though diminished in extent. The period of peace which followed permitted the reigning shah, descendant of Khadjar, to visit Europe, and he has made himself known in the West by his journey and unique volume of travels.

Lustred Pottery.—The art of lustring is, so far as known, of Persian origin, but of ancient and uncertain date. Numerous Persian lustred fragments have been found in the ruins of Rhei or Rhages, a city several times destroyed and rebuilt near its previous site, until its final destruction by Hulaku Khan, A. D. 1250. The lustred pieces are found chiefly in the oldest parts of the ruins, which date of 200 or more B. C. Pliny, who wrote in the first century A. D., speaks of a substance found in *Karamania*, of which murrhine vases were made, remarkable for their lustres of different hues. This observation alludes probably to Persian lustred pottery; and Chardin, a jeweler, traveler, and diplomatist, who visited Persia in 1666, remarks that the finest Persian pottery was then made in Karamania, at Kirman and Yezd; also at Shiraz, the capital of Persidia, and at Metched, the capital of Bactriana.

Fayence Tiles.—Of the interior decoration of buildings in Persia, with glazed tiles, Ferguson observes: "Europe possesses no specimen of any style of ornamentation comparable with this. The painted plaster of the Alhambra is infinitely inferior, and even the mosaic painted glass of our cathedrals is a very partial and incomplete ornament, compared with the brilliancy of a design pervading the whole building and entirely carried out in the same style." The mosque of Tabreez, of the twelfth century, is covered internally and externally throughout with glazed tiles of brilliant colors, "wrought into the most intricate patterns, and with all the elegance for which the Persians were in all ages remarkable." Monuments of the time of Malik Shah, 1072 A. D.; Hulaku Khan, 1256; Ghazen Khan, 1295, are still to be seen, covered with decorative tiling; also the tomb of Sultanieh, 1303-1316, and that which Soleiman the Great erected for his son, 1544. The tiles were made to conform with the designs of the architect, and with excellent effect.

Much of the fayence, especially that without inscriptions, belongs in general to an earlier period, as shown by the monuments and the illuminations in the remarkable work, the "Shah Nameh," written by Firdusi, in 1009. This celebrated history, in verse, of the ancient kings of Persia, has been translated and republished by M. J. Mohl, of the Institute of France. Many of its ornamental forms are the same as those seen on the fayence.

Persian tiles are sometimes remarkable for size as well as beauty. The South Kensington Museum has specimens twenty-four and thirty-one inches in height, and we read of others in Persia six and eight feet high. The palace of Shah Abbas, at Ispahan, is decorated with historical subjects on tiles twenty inches square, in six different colors, and mixtures of these. The mosque of Ispahan, built by Shah Abbas, 1630, and the dome of Shah Ismael, at Ispahan, 1722, are decorated with fayence.

In Asia Minor the monuments of Sconium (Konieh), 1074 A. D.; the minaret of Nicea, 1389; the tomb of Mahomet I. at Broussa, fourteenth century, are similarly decorated; while at Bagdad the tomb of the children of Ali, 1585, presents domes of glazed gilded brick, and walls with floral ornaments on fayence.

Ornament and Symbolism.—Persian vases and tiles are often decorated with conventional forms to which a symbolical meaning is attached.

The emblematic *sun*, the combating *lion and bull*, symbolizing the eternal conflict of Ormuzd and Ahriman, Good and Evil, are met with; also, the *tulip* (in Persian *tulbend*, or turban), at one time a sacred flower, and later symbolizing love. The conventional *cypress* indicated the aspirations of the soul toward heaven; it was an emblem of the religion of Zoroaster. This great man, according to tradition, brought from paradise a cypress, planted it at Balkh, and inscribed upon it the words,

"Gushtasp has embraced the true religion;" subsequently, the king built around it a temple of jeweled marble, in which he placed a copy of the sacred writings, and this became an object of pilgrimages. The cypress gave its name to the island of Cypre ("Cupressus"), and the Greeks and Romans placed it in their graveyards, and attached its branches to the doors of the deceased, to indicate the departure of the soul heavenward. The *gryphon* is a seer, with the upper half of an eagle and the lower half of a lion. Of the gryphon an Arab manuscript says: "Its feathers shone of every possible hue; not only it knew all things, but predicted the future." The *wyvern*, or dragon, with wings and reptilian tail ending in a barbed spear; the *harpy*, with a woman's head and breast, and the body and legs of a vulture, are common in ancient Persian ornament. Although found in the Homerian legends, they were rarely met in Europe until after the return of the Crusaders, who wove them into their ensigns of heraldry, where they still remain.

The human form is common in works of earlier times, but under the injunctions of the Koran it disappears, or a sort of compromise is made resembling nothing on the earth, nor, so far as known, in it—a monster, part man part dragon; a man's figure with horns and a tail (*see* Fig. 44); a man's body with an elephant's head (Fig. 44); bodies mutilated of a member; a human-faced monkey with asses' ears; a man with the head of a bull, and carrying a club.

The origin of the chimerical figures seen in Egyptian, Assyrian, Chinese, Japanese, Persian, Pompeian, and Raffaelesque decoration, is considered to be a mere effort of the imagination. It would be curious if their origin could be ascribed, through transmission by tradition, to preglacial epochs, when man and the cave-lion lodged in caverns, quarreled over a bone on which both left their mark, or sallied forth to resist jointly the formidable reptiles with which they had to contend alike for the "survival of the fittest."

Among other elements of Persian decoration are conventional figures of the Indian pink, the long-stalked pink, the

PERSIAN ORNAMENTATION.

rose, the purple rose, the hyacinth, five-petaled flowers, the palm, palmette, lily, poppy, sprays of leaves, and peacock ornaments. Vines and grapes appear in the later Persian. The floral ornaments are sometimes embossed; rows of inverted flowers are also seen.

Among more common ornaments are scale-work and lozenge-work, both for grounds and borders, and palmette figures. Vultures, hawks, goldfinches, rabbits, hares, gazelles, dogs, deer, and hawking and hunting scenes, are frequent. Bowls and cups are usually decorated with care, inside and outside.

The arms of the King of Persia—a lion couchant, looking backward at the rising sun—is a favorite; and clouds are introduced as ornaments in Persia as well as China. The Persian *dragon* has cloven hoofs, while that of China and Japan has four claws for the plebeian and five for the imperial.

Scale-work in which each scale is filled in with a flower or some animal, diaper-work with floral centres and borders varying from the most stiff and angular to curved and flowing designs, with sprays of leaves or conventional forms, are met with.

Inscriptions in Cufic of the tenth or twelfth century, in mystic characters, in Pehlevi, in Arabic, are frequent; also, portraits of kings, courtiers, governors, eunuchs, are seen. Caligraphy is highly appreciated in Persia, a single line of the handwriting of Mir, and of recent writers, being valued in that country at two or three pounds sterling.

Some light on the dates of the development of Persian industry may be derived from their textiles. Before the time of Mohammed, Eastern princes wore stuffs wrought with their own portraits. Later, names were substituted. The Saracen kings, the Caliph Saladin, the Moors in Spain, wove names and inscriptions into their wearing-apparel. The *homa*, or tree of life, is met with in Persian, Syrian, and other textiles. The Assyrian eagle became later a Persian, Byzantine, and Saracenic device. The Saracens used both the single and double headed eagle; the latter was adopted by the Emperors of Germany. The Mohammedan prohibition respecting all images was not adhered to either by Persians or Arabs, as parrots, cheetahs, giraffes, gazelles, lions, elephants, hawks, and eagles, are common enough in their textiles.

The treatment of *color* in Persian decoration is usually highly conventional; the harmonies of analogy are used to great advantage. A beautiful turquoise color, and the manner in which sprays of leaves are thrown in a free curve with a graceful, feathery sweep, are characteristic. The color applied to the flowers, leaves, and animals, is frequently treated entirely from the point of view of decorative effect, without regard to the color which the objects have in Nature. Thus blue, violet, red, and gray horses are figured. Salmon-tinted flesh-color is frequent; or the human figure is represented in robes of bright blue or green.

TECHNICAL CHARACTERISTICS OF PERSIAN FAYENCE.

Besides hard and soft porcelain and several varieties of pottery produced in Persia, there is found in abundance a fayence distinguished by its hard, sandy, whitish, creamy body of only moderate cohesion, and hard, brilliant siliceous glaze of great cohesive strength. A piece dipped in boiling water as an experiment was sufficiently softened in the interior to enable a long needle to be stirred in it, and appeared to hold together only by the great strength of the glaze. The strength of the piece was restored by evaporating the water absorbed, and replacing it by a crystallizable siliceous liquid. Brongniart suggests that some of the tiles may be merely slabs of sandstone, enameled, painted, and fired, and gives the following analysis:

A.—Tile from the Great Mosque of Jerusalem, colored in turquoise and blue. Silico-alkaline glaze containing no lead. Body sandy, as follows: Silica 87, alumina and iron 5.5, lime 3, magnesia 0.28, potash 1.2, loss 3.

B.—Tile from the tomb of Mohammed at Medina, colored in blue and green. Glaze containing neither lead nor tin. Body: Silica 90, alumina and iron 4, lime 2, magnesia 0.5, potash and moisture 3, loss 0.5.

PERSIAN BODY AND GLAZE.

The following results are derived from the observations of Colonel Scheill: The Persian body consists of silex 500, a particular earth 65. When fired ten hours, it produces fayence; when fired three hours longer and harder, it becomes translucent and produces porcelain. The glaze for this body is formed of white silex 50, *kaliab* 40. The kaliab is the name given to the ashes of an herbaceous plant growing on salt soil. This mixture is fused in an oven, ground, and applied with the addition of gum-tragacanth, or sirup of raisins. This fusion expels twelve per cent. of volatile elements. Various oxides are added to this composition when colored glazes are desired. Finally, to obtain a sonorous body, silex and some lead-oxide are added to the above mixture of silex and kaliab. The use of these ashes is evidently an economical way of obtaining alkali and silica mixed.

The Persian lapis-blue pieces are made by immersing the

FIG. 40.

entire piece in the liquid blue glaze. The copper lustred pieces resemble in lustre the wares of Malaga and Valencia.

PERSIAN TILE (Fig. 40).—This tile, exhibited in Philadelphia, by the Bazaar of Cairo, is a fine example of Persian siliceous ware. It is executed in two colors, on white ground. The outlines and parts indicated darker are in cobalt-blue. The parts marked with light dots are in copper-green. Side, about eight inches.

PERSIAN TILE (Fig. 41).—This tile, owned by the writer, and bought in Cairo, is a fair example of Persian siliceous ware. The ground is a rich creamy white; the brilliant glaze presents

FIG. 41.

numerous colorless cracks. The design is outlined in black; the parts hatched vertically are cobalt, the lighter hatchings are copper-green, except the centre with three flowers, which is turquoise, and the parts in solid black, which are bright red in relief. This red is by some attributed exclusively to Rhodes; it occurs, however, also in Roumania and Persia. The character of the forms is well adapted for rapid and free execution by the hand. Side, nine and three-quarter inches; thickness, nine-sixteenths of an inch. Hard, strong glaze; fragile, sandy body.

PANEL OF TILES (Fig. 42).—These nine tiles, with Arabic inscriptions, the homa or tree of life, hanging lamps, vase of flowers, the whole circumscribed by a border, form a panel

FIG. 42.

suggesting the entrance to a garden. The outlines are black; cobalt, copper-green, and turquoise, are the only other colors used; the ground is white. The style is Arab, adapted from the Persian. Panel, twenty-four inches square. Exhibited by the Bazaar of Cairo.

LAMP-STAND (Figs. 43 and 44).—Of bronze perforated, and

engraved with figure-subjects in medallions, interlaced with evenly-distributed sprays of leaves and flowers, surrounded by borders of scroll patterns and inscriptions in Arabic or Cufic (?). As in much Oriental work, but little time has been spent in obtaining mere mechanical precision, and the effort of the arti-

FIG. 43.

san has been directed toward producing richness, freedom, and variety of design, and on the whole with a happy effect.

Among the figures are men with elephants' heads, seated in chairs; men with horns and tufted tails; seated man with the head of a dog; man carrying a sheep; long-bearded men; youth seated on the ground, sleeping; man with sleeves spreading out at bottom; also rabbits, birds, doves, geese, dogs. (In medallions, upon another lamp-stand, are also lions, gazelles, and horses.) The base, second and fourth ring, are circular and

DETAILS OF LAMP-STAND. 119

tapering; the first and third are ten-sided. A bell-shaped cap probably surmounted the stem originally, as in analogous examples in the South Kensington Museum. The pair of lamp-stands are the property of Mr. R. M. Hunt, loaned by him to the Metropolitan Museum, New York, and sketched with his permission. Fig. 43 gives the elevation and detail of mouldings. Fig. 44 shows part of the base and lower ring. *Old Persian.* Height, three feet; diameter at base, thirteen inches.

FIG. 44.

BRONZE BOWL, engraved with figures placed in bands. On one band are a crowned warrior mounted, cantering, an antelope following, next a swordsman running; two bearded horsemen galloping, crossing swords and seizing each other mutually by their flowing pointed beards; a turbaned horseman cantering off with a leopard held on the saddle behind him, and followed by a greyhound, *ventre-à-terre*; behind, a mounted bowman aims at him; a man with a long, curved conical cap, kneeling on one knee, with a lion next to him; a man with a dog's head, running; a mounted man drinking out of, or blowing, a horn. Upon other bands are a man kneeling, milking a cow, a monster with tiger's body, the body and arms of a man holding a sword in place of the neck, and the head of an ox. The figures show some curious details of costume. Diameter, six inches.

Fig. 45 presents a selection of ornaments in different styles. In the *Persian* panel the border is from a Persian manuscript in the British Museum, the centre from a Persian manufacturer's pattern-book in the South Kensington Museum; the *Indian* border is from lacquer-work, the centre from a fabric in the South Kensington Museum; the *Arabian* border is from a copy of the Koran in the mosque of Barkooyeh, 1384 A. D., the centre from the mosque of Sultan Kaloon, 1284 A. D.; the *Moresque* border and centre from the Alhambra; the *Byzantine* from Sancta Sophia, Constantinople; the *Venetian* from St. Mark's mosaics, with a narrow panel from Monreale, Sicily, eleventh century; the *Early Italian* from various pieces of earthenware—all the above are given more fully, and in colors, in Owen Jones's "Grammar of Ornament;" the *Gothic* (from Fergusson) border from Prior de Estria's screen in Canterbury Cathedral, and from the tomb of Bishop Marshall, Exeter Cathedral, the centre from Lichfield Cathedral and various mediæval illuminated manuscripts.

Although, in deriving ornament from Nature, the same forms may be arrived at independently by various artists, it appears nevertheless probable that much that is looked upon as Gothic, for instance, is derived directly from the Byzantine, Moresque, and Persian, and that each style is developed out of pre-existing styles, by gradual steps and the addition of certain original elements.

Reproductions of Persian Fayence.—Minton and Maw, in England, have produced mechanical copies of Persian patterns handsome in effect, but lacking the variety of hand-

COMPARISON OF VARIOUS STYLES. 121

Fig. 45.

painted work. Doulton has attained this element, but is comparatively deficient in harmony of color. Parvillée and Collinot, in France, have done well. Upon a white or colored ground Collinot scatters lightly flowers, imparting relief by repeated superposition of enamels, circumscribed by a dark copper composition, which in firing forms a metallic outline to every flower, and prevents the thick enamel from spreading. Collinot uses as models the drawings brought back by Adalbert de Beaumont from his travels. Deck's work, though often crackled, is artistic. The delicacy of the Persian contrasts of color has, however, not yet been equaled.

Thus, a balance between the low orange-red and the blues and greens, toned down by an India-ink color which circles in delicate spirals of smoke-gray, heightening and purifying the other colors, on a creamy white or colored ground; an absence of mechanical hardness of outline; not uniformity, but fluctuation of color; not spotty contrasts, but a beautiful analogous series of colors, beginning with green, passing through turquoise-blue to a pure deep cobalt, and thence to a lilac hue: these are some of the delicacies of Persian decoration that have not been attained in Europe.

Messrs. Owen Jones, Eastlake, Dresser, and Sheddon, have lately made designs in England in the Persian style.

PERSIAN GROUP.

There are wares known as Damascus, Rhodian, and Anatolian. Their ornamental forms are so entirely Persian in character that they are sometimes called by that name, and to distinguish them there is little but the technical execution of the pieces. It is, however, desirable to keep them separate, as no doubt, when larger collections are made, a proper study of their decoration may lead to interesting distinctive features. The writer cannot, however, with C. D. Fortnum, group these wares, including the Persian, in one family, under the name of "Damascus" or "Damas." An appropriate name for such a group is "Persian," since that alone would truly indicate the origin of the ornamental forms and most of the technical processes seen in these wares.

RHODIAN.

History.—The island of Rhodes, forty-five miles long by eighteen wide, derived its name from a *rose*, which was its symbol. It was colonized by the Dorians, who worshiped at the sanctuary of Apollo. This divinity, peculiar to the Doric race, and worshiped at the Thessalian Tempe, Delphi, Crete, in Asia Minor and in Greece, and later at Rome in 430 B. C., was identified by Virgil and others with Helios, the sun. Indeed, Apollo is said to have been born in light, and the Colossus of Rhodes was a representation of Helios; so that it would appear that the Dorians were in one sense sun-worshipers. At an early period they sent out colonies to Italy, Sicily, and Spain.

After the Persian War Rhodes belonged to the Athenian confederacy. Rhodes was built in B. C. 408, chiefly by Hippodamus, the architect of the Piræus of Athens, and became celebrated for its splendor and works of art. In B. C. 412 the Rhodians deserted the Athenians, and in B. C. 357 fought against Athens. Memnon, a Rhodian, under the Persian king, defended in vain the island against Alexander; but after his death they opposed the Athenians again, and heroically resisted the Macedonians, B. C. 303. The Colossus of Rhodes was prostrated B. C. 224. At this time the Rhodians were sovereigns of the sea and friends of Rome, but in B. C. 42 Cassius plundered the island.

In 616 A. D. Chosroes, the Persian king, conquered the island from the Romans. Later, it was recovered by the Byzantine Empire, about 746, and belonged successively to the Venetians, Greeks, Genoese, and Turks, until, in 1308, the Emperor Emanuel granted the island to the Knights of St. John. In 1480 Mahomet II. besieged Rhodes, without success; but in 1522 the Knights of St. John capitulated to the Turks, led by Solyman II., and retired to Malta, since which time Rhodes has belonged to Turkey.

The Rhodian pottery greatly resembles the Persian, and the Persian prisoners held by the Rhodians undoubtedly manufactured some of the wares, as on one piece is seen a Persian captive lifting his arms to heaven for deliverance.

Characteristics.—The body is whitish-gray and sandy, the glaze hard and siliceous. Both are coarser than the Persian or Damascus; the decoration is more gaudy and less harmonious than the old Persian; the enamels are also more in relief, and especially a bright iron-red pigment used in relief is sometimes exclusively attributed to Rhodes, but is also found on the Persian. The conventional treatment and floral forms are also Persian in character. Besides animals and birds, Rhodian ships and coats of arms appear, and when these are introduced they serve to distinguish the wares which were mostly made during the fifteenth and sixteenth centuries.

Among the subjects represented on Rhodian pottery are: Flowers and sprays springing from one bunch; green and red trefoils; white and blue tulips on red ground; often borders of black scrolls on blue and white; grotesque, human-headed animals; three-masted ships of the fifteenth century; ships traced in black, with blue sails.

ANATOLIAN.

A manufactory is known at Kutahia, the capital of Anatolia. Small pieces with a rough glaze gayly decorated, with less matured taste than the Persian, using a brilliant yellow, incised hatchings, and flowers, etc., are believed to have been made there. Also pretty incense-burners, with a bright decoration resembling the Cashmere stuffs, are known to come from Kutahia.

DAMASCUS.

History.—Damascus, which after 740 B. C. belonged to the Assyrians, passed successively to the Persians; to the Greeks, 332 B. C.; to the Romans, 70 B. C.; Saracens, A. D. 633. Damascus belonged to the Mussulmans after 1075 A. D. It was besieged by the Crusaders in 1148, but withstood them.

Tamerlane, in 1401, massacred all its inhabitants excepting the armorers. The city belonged afterward to the Mamelukes. Sultan Selim I. conquered it in 1516. From 1833 to 1840 it was governed by the Viceroy of Egypt, when it was restored to Turkey.

Under this class may be included the fayence of Syria, Asia Minor, and Roumania, until the character of these wares is separately studied.

Characteristics.—The body is of a grayish, creamy white, of sandy texture, and the glaze hard and siliceous, much resembling the Persian ware, while the decorative ornaments are entirely derived from the Persian.

It is interesting to note here that the art of damascening steel, first known in Europe from Damascus, has long been known in Persia, and is carried on at the present day in great perfection at Ispahan.

As an occasional distinctive feature of Damascus ware may be named a dull-purple color used against blue, a sage-green, and a turquoise used in connection with two shades of blue.

In the Exhibition of 1867 was a collection of fayence from Roumania. The character resembled the Persian, and presented the feature also seen on Byzantine jewelry, of grading or blending the color of the enamel in each cloison, as from green to yellow, from blue to white, from violet to lilac. These blended colors are seen on Roumanian wares, circumscribed by a thick black enamel line which almost forms a cloison, and placed on a blue ground. These colors differ from the early Persian enamels, which are usually fluid and paler. The blending, however, is seen also repeatedly in Chinese and Hindoo decoration.

A hanging-lamp is known, dated 1549, made for the mosque of the Dome of the Rock of Jerusalem, and signed by *The painter, the poor, the humble Mustafa.*

Fayence eggs, serving to terminate the chains of hanging-lamps, are found in Asia Minor. Some have the Christian emblems of a Byzantine cross and cherubim upon them.

SICILIAN.

It will assist in the researches on Sicilian ware to bear in mind the principal points in the history of the island.

History.—The name of the island was originally *Sicania*, or *Trinacria*, from its triangular shape. The *Sicanians* are said by Thucydides to have come from Iberia. From the plains of Latium came a people, the *Sicules*, driven back by the Umbrians. The Sicules retired across the straits about 1280 B. C., gradually wrested the possession of the island from the Sicanians, and changed its name to *Sicily*.

At an early period, when Carthage was in its infancy, the Phœnicians colonized Sicily. They were followed by the Greeks and Chalcidians under Theocles, who founded Syracuse about 734 B. C. Thucydides has described the subsequent attempts of the Athenians, about 400 B. C., to conquer the Dorians at Syracuse. They sent against them Demosthenes and others, who finally, aided by the Carthaginians, obtained for this people a foothold on the island, and, in 383 B. C., divided it between the Sicilians and Carthaginians. Later, the Sicilians, aided by Pyrrhus I., and subsequently, in 264 B. C., by the Romans, ultimately drove away the Africans, but only to fall themselves under the power of Rome, and in 212 B. C. Sicily was made a Roman province. At the end of this period, A. D. 470 to 536, the island was overrun alternately by the Goths and Vandals; when Belisarius took possession in the name of the Emperor of the East.

About 651 or 665 A. D., the Mohammedan Arabs from Egypt began expeditions against Sicily, of which, after two centuries of their system of warfare, or *razzias*, they took complete possession.

From the Arab works of Ebn-Kaldoun and Ebn-el-Athir, on the "History of Africa under the Aglabites, and of Sicily under the Mussulmans," may be gathered the incidents of this rule.

Aghlab-Ibrahim-ben-Abdallah took the government of Sicily

in hand Anno Hegira 217; Abou-el-Aghlab followed in 236 A. H.; Abbas-ben-Ferrara drove the Greeks finally, with small exceptions, from Sicily, 244 A. H., from which dates a regular Arab government. His son Abdallah was elected by the Arabs in Sicily, but the Aglabite emir Abou-Ibm-Ahmed sent instead his lieutenant, Khafadja-ben-Sofian, to rule, 248 A. H.; he was assassinated 255 A. H. His son Mohamet, who succeeded, was likewise assassinated by eunuchs, 257 A. H. The Emir of Africa sent as his successor Ahmed-ben-Jacoub-ben-Salmah, who, in 264 A. H., captured Syracuse, where an ounce of bread had become worth an ounce of gold; it was pillaged and burned, and the spoils carried to Palermo; Syracuse never recovered, and the modern town consists of but one-quarter of the old town.

The "holy wars," as the Arabs denominated their attacks upon the Greeks, continued under Djafar, El-Abbas, El-Fadhl, and Hocain, who died 271 A. H. Then came El-Tennimi and Aboul-Abbas the Aglabite from Africa; then his father, Ibrahim, who destroyed Taormine; then M. Sarcoussi, and his son Ali. Dissensions in Africa occurred 297 A. H., when El-Hassan attempted to govern Sicily, but he was of the sect of Ali, and the Sicilian Arabs, who were of the sect of Abbas, under Ahmed-ben-Koreb, drove him off; later the Abbassides were in turn overcome by Abou-Saïd and Selim-ben-Reschid, who reëstablished in power the sect of Ali, 313 A. H., and also pillaged Calabria in Italy. Dissensions followed, fomented by Constantine and the Greeks, but in 341 A. H. came the rule of Ahmed and seventy years of peace at home, which saw the erection of fine *Arab monuments*. In 354 A. H. the Arabs celebrated, as important, the victory of Medjaz against the Greek Empire in Sicily. Abou-Cacem-Ali, his successor, invaded Calabria, and defeated Otto II., 372 A. H., who was on his way to attack the Emperor of the East. Djafar-ben-Mohammed and Abdallah (375) bring us to the most prosperous era of Arab government in Sicily—that of Thikat-el-Daoulet-Abou-el-Foutouh, in 379 A. H. His son Djafar (388) and grandson El-Akhal (410) followed, but the Sicilian Arabs, tired of their Obeyidite governors, called in the Zereids, and decapitated El-Akhal in 417; they soon repented, and called in his brother, El-Samsam. Dissensions arose, he was driven out by Ebn-el-Thamoun, who established himself in power. The cruelty of this governor to his wife caused him to be defeated by her brother Ebn-el-Houasch, whereupon, 1060 A. D., he treacherously called in the aid of the Norman Roger, who invaded Sicily with success, and later, with the aid of a Pisan fleet, seized Palermo, 1071 A. D., and the government of Sicily.

Two centuries before that, the Moslems had as usual offered to the vanquished Sicilians the choice between paying tribute or embracing the faith of Mohammed. The Abbé Maurolico mentions that in public ceremonies at Messina two standards were unfurled: one, the Saracen, with a black tower on a green ground; the other, the Christian, with a gold cross embroidered on a red ground. The Arabs introduced the culture of cotton and sugar-cane, the use of siphon-aqueducts, and of silk embroidery, as shown by a cloak ordered by the Norman Roger, and taken to Nuremberg by Henry VI. in 1196; it is like those worn by the rulers of Sicily, with a long, embroidered Cufic inscription, and the date 528 of the Hegira.

Neither under the Normans was Mohammedanism proscribed, but it paid tribute. Roger, who adopted the name of Count of Sicily, died 1101 A. D. His son, William I., followed; then Roger II., who united Sicily and Naples, under the name of the kingdom of the Two Sicilies, in 1131. William II. followed; Henry VI. of Germany, who died 1197; and Frederick II. The Arabs, who were at first treated amicably, were by degrees persecuted; they rebelled and were defeated, and many were sent to *Nocera*, on the continent, and forbidden to return.

Frederick II., Emperor of Germany, died in 1250. His son Conrad fought against Pope Innocent VI. and took Naples, but died there, and the ambitious Manfred was crowned in 1258 at Palermo. Charles I. of Anjou, named successor by Pope Urban IV., defeated Manfred, and the French conquered Sicily in 1266. In 1282 the massacre of the French at Palermo occurred, and spread over the island, destroying some eight thousand men, women, and children. From 1282 to 1409, the house of Aragon gave as rulers Peter I., James, Frederick II. of Aragon, Peter II., Louis, Frederick III., Mary, and Martin; in 1409 it was annexed to the crown of Aragon, when internal dissensions broke out. In 1501 Ferdinand of Castile was called in, and thenceforward Sicily belonged either to Spain or to the Bourbon kingdom of Naples.

SICULO-PERSIAN.

Wares found in Sicily, closely resembling the Persian by the ornamental forms and the texture of the body and glaze, are properly distinguished by the name of Siculo-Persian. They may have been imported; but as the Arabs established the same industry elsewhere, these may be attributed to the Arabs during their stay in Sicily, from 651 to about 1200 A. D. Perhaps they should be ascribed more particularly to the prosperous reigns, 960 to 1040 A. D.

The ornaments upon Sicilian textiles throw a valuable light upon the dates of different styles of Arab manufactures in that island. Three distinct periods are noticed: the first, preceding the Norman Roger in 1071 A. D., in which African animals, the giraffe, antelope, gazelle, lion, elephant, and the Indian parrot and leopard, or cheetah, are found woven in the stuffs, together with some Arabic word; the second, dating from the time when Roger, who had taken Corinth, Athens, and Thebes, carried captive to Palermo silk-weavers, who impressed a Byzantine element upon the Saracenic ornamentation, such as grotesque masks and the Greek cross; the third, in which the cross and Christian emblems are woven in with Mohammedan elements. This third style, according to some, coincides with the accession of the house of Aragon, in 1282. From what Maurelico says, however, it may be of an earlier period.

Characteristics.—The body is sandy, of a creamy, whitish tone, and of moderate cohesion. The glaze is transparent and hard, with a greenish tinge. The firing is at a high temperature, as shown by the hard glaze which has sometimes run into drops at the bottom of the ware. The painting on these pieces is black and blue, directly upon the body, and glazed over. The drawing is archaic. Arabic inscriptions are found.

Another variety has a dark-purplish-blue vitreous glaze, over which a lustred scroll ornament is applied. The body, glazes, and lustres, are different from the Siculo-Moresque pieces. The lustre is rich, brilliant, and of a fine texture.

Upon contemporary Sicilian textiles are found animals half elephant half griffin; eagles perched in pairs with a radiating sun between them; dogs in pairs, running, with their heads turned back; running harts with a leg tied to the neck and an eagle swooping down; a hart with its tail in the last link of a chain fastened to its neck. The swan also, gracefully drawn, is a favorite with the Sicilians. Harts and demi-dogs, both with very large wings and long manes streaming far behind them; harts lodged under green trees with a paling about; vine and parsley leaves, are also seen.

Of the third period are harts with the letter M floriated, and winged lions, crosses floriated, crosses sprouting out on two sides with *fleurs-de-lis*, and four-legged monsters, some winged, biting their tails. The Sicilians, probably after the Crusades, were particularly fond of heraldic charges—wyverns, eagles, lions rampant, griffins, etc.

OVOID VASE, OF PERSIAN STYLE (Fig. 46).—Decorated with three antelopes among leaves, stepping over rocks, with Arabic inscriptions on the neck and foot. The outlines are traced in brownish black on the white ground in a free but primitive style. The leaves are suggested with ornamental effect in a manner which allows of rapid execution. Dots of dark blue are sown over the antelopes and leaves, and the rocks are touched with blue. The hard firing and nature of the glaze have caused the blue to diffuse itself downward, thus aiding the appearance of the hairy coat of the gazelles. The body has a buff, sandy texture; it has been coated with a clay or stanniferous wash, and, after painting, the whole has been dipped in a brilliant, thick siliceous glaze, which runs into drops at the bottom of the piece, and presents a greenish tinge under a certain thickness, and occasional distinct cracks. The

FIG. 46.

potting, though not mechanically accurate on the surface, has nevertheless produced a graceful form. Found at Palermo. Height, twelve and a half inches. No. 1 of Signor Castellani's collection.

OVOID VASE, OF PERSIAN STYLE (Fig. 47).—Decorated with four peacocks outlined in black and touched up with blue, and outlines of six-petaled flowers and pointed foliage or trefoils;

SICULO-PERSIAN.

with parts in low-relief, produced by painting under the glaze, with an opaque enamel whiter than the remainder of the ground, and resulting in an undulated surface. The siliceous glaze is thick and most brilliant; it gives a general faint greenish tinge to the piece, presents numerous fine brown cracks

FIG. 47.

and a quartz-like appearance near the foot. In other ways this valuable piece resembles the preceding; the blue, however, is darker and thicker, and has run downward farther in the firing. Also from Palermo. Height, twelve and a quarter inches. No. 2.

OVOID VASE (Fig. 48).—Decorated with arabesques of copper lustre on a blue ground. This vase has been coated inside and out with a hard blue enamel, which, on inspection, appears faintly marbled in places by unequal distribution, and presents on the outside numerous light specks faintly lustred in violet or green, and also sandy specks. The well-distributed orna-

FIG. 48.

mentation is in copper lustre, in a scroll-pattern derived from the Persian, and resembling those also on Rhodian pieces. The lustre varies from a brassy hue, through copper and brown, to violet. The effect is rich and harmonious. From Sicily. Height, six and a half inches. No. 6.

SICULO-MORESQUE.

This ware resembles, by its body, earthy or stanniferous wash, copper lustre, and by the character of the ornamental forms, the Hispano-Moresque wares of Malaga and Valencia.

134 SICULO-MORESQUE.

It appears not unlikely that they were made partly while Sicily belonged to the house of Aragon, and the Moors were all-powerful in Spain, from 1282 to 1409, but chiefly by the Moors, who fled from persecution in Spain and also took refuge in Majorca and in Italy from about 1500 to 1700 A. D.; and that they are in general of later date than the Hispano-Moresque wares. Examples have been found at Catala Girone.

Characteristics.—An ordinary clay body, a clay slip or stanniferous wash, glazed and lustred, with a lustre of a coppery hue. Sometimes also a rich blue glaze is applied and lustred.

LARGE BOWL, WITH FOOT (Fig. 49).—The body, coated

FIG. 49.

with a white stanniferous enamel, has been fired, and decorated with a copper lustre in spiral and floral forms, evenly balanced and rapidly applied, and varying from a brassy hue to reddish purple in reflected light. The enamel is of a grayish, creamy white, thick, moderately glossy, and speckled. The effect of the decoration is highly pleasing. From Sicily. Height, ten and a half inches; diameter, fourteen inches. No. 7a.

MAJORCAN.

Majorca, one of the Balearic Isles, is sixty miles long, twenty-three wide, and presents a mountain-peak five thousand one hundred and twenty feet high.

Carthage began the conquest of these islands by that of Iviza about 663 B. C., and captured others during the next two centuries. The inhabitants were proficient in the use of the sling; and their next conquerors, the Romans, and notably Cæsar, employed them under the name of "fundæ librales," from their slinging stones weighing one pound. The Romans named the islands Majorca and Minorca from their size.

In 426 A. D. the Vandals took possession. In 798 A. D. the Moors followed, and formed in 1009 a separate kingdom of the Balearic Isles. Their character was piratical. For a time Charlemagne drove the Moors away, but they returned.

The Pisans fitted out an expedition and obtained a victory over the Majorcans in 1115. Pope Pascal II. combated them, and Don Jayme, King of Aragon, expelled the Moors in 1232; but Minorca remained in their hands till 1285. He put his third son on the throne, which remained separate till 1349, when it reverted to Spain. In 1521 the peasants massacred the nobles. Count Villars subjugated Minorca in 1707, and Majorca in 1715; and later, in the Peninsular War, the Majorcans sided with Spain against the French. In the fourteenth century there was much commerce between Spain, Majorca, and Italy.

Gio. di Bernardi, writing in 1422, mentions the large sale in Italy of fayence from Majorca and Minorca. Iviza is also mentioned by Vargas in 1787, as having ceased to produce its celebrated fayence.

Ynca is the site of a factory of which a piece of ware with the arms of the town, and a red ruby lustre, exists in the Musée de Cluny, probably of the fifteenth century. Scaliger, writing about 1550, speaks in high praise of Majolica, adding, "We call them *majolica*, changing one letter in the name of the Balearic island, where we are assured the most beautiful are made."

Characteristics.—Besides the arms of the town of Ynca (which are: paly gules and or, on a fess argent; a dog in the act of bounding, sable), there are arabesques and fern-leaf decorations, and the pieces are beautifully coated with a nacreous lustre.

Later pieces have shields of arms introduced.

Majorca contains mines of lead, iron, and cinnabar. As these three ingredients, according to Piccolpasso, enter into the formation of the lustres, these mines must have facilitated the production of the lustred wares on that island.

HISPANO-MORESQUE.

History.—The name *Iberia* given to Spain is of Greek origin, meaning west of Italy and Greece. *Hispania* is of Carthaginian or Phœnician origin. About 1000 B. C. the Phœnicians planted colonies in Spain; after 500 B. C. the Carthaginians held part of the country by conquest. The Romans followed, 206 B. C.; then the Vandals, Alans, and Goths, 400 A. D. The Visigoths took complete possession, 500 A. D. In 712 the Moors entered Cordova, and drove the Goths to another part of the country, where they founded the kingdom of Oviedo, which became subsequently that of Leon. In 756 Abd-el-Rhama, at the head of his Saracens, established the caliphate of Cordova, and erected a mosque there, decorated with wall-tiles in Arab style; his kingdom was bounded by the Douro and Ebro, while Charlemagne held all to the north of this line.

In the twelfth century internal dissensions divided the Moors into the separate kingdoms of Saragossa, Murcia, Jaen, Valencia, Seville, Cordova, Granada, Toledo, Lisbon, Tortosa, and Almeria; and the King of Leon, profiting by these dissensions, took the kingdom of Toledo. In 1248 the Alhambra was erected by Mohammed-ibn-Alhamar, the *azulejos* or tiles of which bear the inscription, *There is none strong but God.*

Ferdinand III. united the kingdoms of Leon and Castile, and conquered from the Moors the kingdoms of Cordova in 1230; Jaen, 1242; Seville, 1248; Murcia, 1250; while the King of Aragon, in 1229, conquered Valencia, and then Majorca, Sicily in 1295, Sardinia in 1325, Naples in 1435. Ferdinand the Catholic, by his marriage with Isabella, in 1479, joined the crowns of Aragon and Castile; the Christians thus united under him conquered the Moors in 1492, and began the work of conversion—Cardinal Ximenes, in his zeal, baptizing as many as three thousand Mohammedans in one day in 1506. A royal decree, in 1566, proscribed the use of the Moorish language, dress, bath, ornamentation, books, and dancing—everything almost except their persons; this was left for Philip III., who, in 1610, ordered the expulsion of all Mohammedans, and six hundred thousand souls left for Majorca, Italy, and other parts, where the knowledge and talent of their artisans were appreciated and received remuneration.

The researches of Baron Davillier have done much to clear up the dates and localities of the manufacture of lustred fayence by the Moors in Spain.

Señor Rivadeneyra, who traveled recently in Persia, mentions a document assigning the town of Rioja, in Spain, to the Persians as their place of residence, showing the existence of Persians (doubtless artisans) in Spain.

MALAGA.

This town, founded by the Phœnicians, was taken by the Arabs, 714 A. D., and held by them until the Spaniards retook it in 1487.

From a Moorish source, the memoirs of the travels of Ibn-Batoutah, of Tangiers, written about 1350, we learn that "at Malaga is manufactured the beautiful pottery or golden porcelain which is exported to the farthest countries."

Lucio Marineo, who chronicles the reign of Ferdinand and Isabella, mentions the beautiful fayence still made at Malaga in 1517. It is believed that subsequently the manufacture at Malaga declined, while that of Valencia increased in importance.

Characteristics.—The arabesque decoration of the Moors shows abundantly the Persian origin of its forms, which they modified in a manner characteristic of themselves, and distributed with a more geometrical and mechanical order over the surface.

The earlier pieces have a paler and more golden lustre, while the later ones present a redder lustre and are somewhat coarser in design, and Christian inscriptions and coats of arms appear.

The inscriptions on the azulejos of the Alhambra are of three sorts: *Ayat*, that is, verses from the Koran; *Asja*, that is, pious sentences not from the Koran; *Ashar*, that is, poems in praise of those who erected the palace. The first two kinds of inscriptions are in Cufic characters, and often arranged ornamentally so as to read equally from right to left or from left to right, or up and down. The modern Arabic handwriting, which came into use 950 A. D., did not at first supplant the Cufic, which continued in use till 1508.

Where the inscribed tiles are found in pavements, they have not been placed there by the Arabs, as good Mohammedans avoid stepping even on accidental scraps of paper, lest they should contain the name of Allah.

The well-known Alhambra vase is attributed to Malaga, about 1320 or 1350. It is decorated in blue-and-gold lustre, on a whitish, somewhat flesh-colored body, with arabesques and panels on which two antelopes are figured.

A vase with large, flat, scollop-shaped handles, covered throughout with a diaper pattern of trellised vine-leaves, tendrils, and small flowers, in brownish-golden lustre, and blue upon a white ground, is attributed to Malaga.

VALENCIA.

The manufacture of a jasper-red pottery, employing twelve hundred men, at *Saguntum*, in the kingdom of Valencia, is mentioned by Pliny. We have seen that after the Romans came the Goths, then the Arabs in 711 A. D. In 1000 A. D. Valencia became the capital of the Moorish kingdom. Then the Christians, under Jayme I. the Conqueror, took possession, in 1239, of the kingdom of Valencia, and extended a license for potting to the Saracens of *Xativa*. In this century a university was founded here, and revived in the fifteenth.

In 1455 the Venetian Senate prohibits the importation of all earthenware "except crucibles and majolica of *Valencia*."

Lucio Marineo, in 1517, speaks of the high esteem in which are held the Valencia wares "which are so well gilded;" and Capmany, in 1528, cites an ordinance of Barcelona which mentions the exportation of fayence of Valencia.

Martin de Vicayana, in 1564, in his *Cronica de Valencia*, mentions the towns of *Biar* and *Trayguera*, in that province, as having many potteries making dishes and large vases.

Escolano, in 1610, further adds to the list of Valencian potteries the towns of *Paterna*, Bourg d'Alaquaz, *Manises*, and also *Quartæ*, *Carcre*, and *Villalonga*.

In 1530 Antonio Beuter mentions all these places for their clay, except Manises; while Escolano praises the Manises ware, and says it is sent to Italy in exchange for Pisan fayence.

In 1613 Fr. Diago speaks of the copper-lustred roofing tiles of Paterna and Carcre, and praises the painting of Manises ware, adding that "the pope, cardinals, and princes, send hither for them."

The dates of the Moresque-Valencian wares are probably from 1239 to about 1613. One piece, dated 1610, is known. At about this period the copper lustre only is retained, and the ornament changes from Moorish to Spanish and rococo.

In 1780 Talbot Dillon mentions the copper-colored gilded fayence then made at Manises.

140   HISPANO-MORESQUE.

In 1801 Fischer also mentions them; and later again Davillier comes across an hotel-keeper who also makes lustred pottery.

The firm of Pickman & Co., of Seville, make at the present day azulejos with impressed patterns and coarse metallic lustre.

Characteristics.—M. Davillier remarks that St. John the Evangelist is held in particular esteem at Valencia. The first sentence of his Gospel, "In principio erat Verbum, et Verbum erat apud Deum," on a banderole carried in the mouth of an eagle with spread wings, is found on Valencia ware. The eagle alone, with open wings, is also his symbol, and appears on some pieces, on the face or on the reverse; while the eagle inscribed in an heraldic escutcheon forms the arms of the kingdom of Aragon. An old church named after St. Catharine exists at Valencia; and a vase with the inscription *Santa Catalina guarda nos*, in Gothic letters, as well as a vase with a drawing of St. Catharine, is attributed to Valencia; also a golden-lustred vase with armorial bearings, grotesque decoration, and stopper, and a plateau with the eagle and a trellised vine-leaf diaper. This vine-leaf diaper, executed in golden lustre and blue, is often met on Valencian ware.

BARCELONA AND OTHER POTTERIES.

This town, named after Hamilcar Barca, the father of Hannibal, and who rebuilt it 233 B. C., was an independent city 864 A. D., and incorporated with Aragon in 1164.

In 1491 Hieronymus Paulus, in his *Hispania Illustrata*, says of the fayence of Barcelona that it had long been esteemed and sought even at Rome; while Bareyros, a Portuguese, praises Barcelona ware as superior even to Valencian.

In the garden, in Arab style, of the palace of the *Real-Audiencia*, built in 1436, are to be seen fayence-pieces, examples of this ware. From the statements of Marineo Siculo, it appears that *Murcia, Morviedro, Toledo,* and *Talavera, Jael* and *Teruel* in Aragon, also had potteries.

NICULOSO FRANCISCO'S PICTURE, ON TILES (Fig. 50).—

NICULOSO FRANCISCO, OF PISA.

This picture, executed on about ninety-nine tiles, in the chapel of Ferdinand and Isabella, in the Alcazar at Seville, has been carefully copied in oil-colors on canvas, and the copy has been exhibited in Philadelphia, by Spain. The subject appears to be the meeting of Mary and Elizabeth. The embroidery of

FIG. 50.

the stuffs resembles the Moresque ornaments on Malaga lustred ware, and shows its Persian affiliation. The colors chiefly used are yellow, blue, violet, green, and black. The inscription, NICVLVSO FRANCISCO ITALIANO M. E. FECIT, is near the bottom. A border, not shown on the sketch, about two tiles wide, surrounds the picture; on it, at the top, are the Mother and Child, with flaming rays, and *Manases* on a label, which may indicate Manises as the place of manufacture. On the sides are dignitaries variously attired, with crowns, turbans, or hoods, and the names *Asna* (?), *Roboan, Alanor, David, Ioatama, Iorama, Obias*. At the bottom is a turbaned, reclining, and bearded figure, inscribed *Jese V.* The picture within this frame presents a low arch at the top, upheld by two flying Cupids.

The painter is the Niculoso Francisco, of Pisa, who is known to have worked in Spain, and decorated the church of Santa Paolo, at Seville, with Della-Robbian bass-reliefs. Fortnum mentions (p. 475) a work with the same inscription, and the date 1504, in the Capilla de Azulejos, in the Alcazar of Seville.

Among the devices and subjects found upon various Hispano-Moresque pieces are the following:

A ship in full sail, the sail bearing the royal shield of Portugal; simulated Arabic inscriptions, a gryphon on the reverse; the arms of Aragon impaled with quarterly Leon and Castile, concentric lustre circles on reverse; a lion rampant on a gold field sown with stars; a shield bearing—sable, two lion's-paws erased, in saltire beneath a chess-rook, or; shield of arms in blue bearing quarterly a cross *pátée*, and barry indented; diapered leaf-ornaments are frequent; a shield bearing a bull, an antelope, and some leaves in dark-blue outline; a party-colored floriated cross borne by a dove; a bouquet of pinks springing from a vase; a bird among foliage; a wyvern with outspread wings; a bird carrying a fruit; geometric star-roundels; a gryphon and Catholic inscription in Spanish.

Among the inscriptions are: *Ave Maria gra. plena; Cum sis yn mensa vino de paupere pensa*—that is, "When at table and at wine, think of the poor."

ART.

Of the many who have attempted to define art, few agree entirely in their conclusions. Even when the sense of the word is limited to the fine arts, some discrepancies prevail, for which a sufficient reason may readily be found.

Art in a general sense is, to a large extent, an expression of feeling. No one's feelings are always the same, and no two individuals, perhaps, ever feel exactly alike. If two painters undertake to represent the same subject, they will paint it differently, each in conformity with his own feelings. So with spectators. The opinions of each in relation to a work of art will conform to his respective feelings, which, like the expressions of the human countenance, are never identical in different persons.

The premises being unlike, the conclusions are unlike, and in these diverse and variable sources of opinion some explanation may be found of the disagreements regarding particular works of art, and of the discords in the definitions.

Nevertheless, something may be said in a general sense that will meet, perhaps, with little dissent.

Most writers on the subject agree in this, that fine art consists partly in imitations of Nature as reflected in the human mind, and partly in the expression of things not embodied in visible Nature, but existing in the mind in ideal types of things.

"Art," says Aristotle, "must imitate a double Nature, that within and that without itself; art is the expression of thought by the imitation of Nature," and "painting should represent not what is but what should be; poetry is truer than history;" and Bacon defines art as "man added to Nature."

In considering the aims and methods, we find that art appeals to human feelings and intelligence, and aims to please, to instruct, to elevate, and to embellish social and domestic life. Heart, sensibility, imagination, intelligence, and genius, are requisites of true art; and works which embody the feelings and yearnings, the common sentiments and common sense of the people, awaken responsive emotions and sympathies, and are effective and grand.

Harmony is the central element of each division of art. Sculpture is harmony of forms; painting is harmony of forms and colors; music is harmony of sounds.

The artist strives to express in his work the high ideal of his subject which exists in his mind. In so doing he studies closely the forms and imitates the ways of Nature in her apparent efforts to the same end. The ideal must be true to Nature, for an exaggerated ideal which ceases to be true becomes unnatural and awakens no approving response.

Art is obviously a form of language, and the true function of each division of art is to express what cannot be so well expressed by any other mode.

The contemplation of the ideal and the study of the beautiful are elevating and refining; but culture and refinement are compatible with many vices, and the character of the influence of art depends upon the moral or immoral tone that pervades it.

The impression is common that success in art depends entirely upon superior natural gifts; that to achieve distinction one must be born with artistic faculties above the ordinary level. Some pretend that science and diversified studies are unfavorable to the best development of the art-talent, and they add that Raphael was illiterate, and his letters full of grammatical errors. Renan remarks that "beautiful works are not made to order," and suggests "the double impossibility of imparting originality to those who have none, and of disciplining those who have." But incomplete views of this kind should have little weight. Doubtless, there are various grades of art-talent, and instances of brilliant genius, but no faculty is more universal than that of feeling and appreciating the influence of art, and none more common than the talent required to produce artistic work, which, like other endowments, depends for quality and strength upon cultivation and development.

The influence of art is not limited to the range of high art. It finds a larger field in the modified and diffused forms in which it blends with the necessary and useful, and embellishes the surroundings of ordinary domestic life. The useful is better for being beautiful. Industrial and decorative art are inseparable from each other in high civilization. Our dwellings, our utensils, persons, surroundings, are within their scope. We are made happier by the presence of objects that display thought, skill, taste, genius, and beauty; and every child of the humblest artisan or laborer has that in him which, properly developed, is capable of contributing to these conditions.

The maxims which Confucius gathered from ancient traditions suggest another point of view from which art may be profitably studied. In the *Ta-Hio*, or "Great Study," we find that "the law of the Great Study, or of practical philosophy, consists in developing and bringing back to light the luminous principle of reason which we have received from heaven, in renovating men, and in placing our final aim in perfection, or the sovereign good."

Also, that "the beings of Nature have a cause and effects; human actions have a cause and consequences; to know causes and effects, principles and consequences, is to approach very near to the rational method by which perfection is to be attained." Let us examine in this analytic spirit.

Art, derived from *ars, artis*, skill in joining, retains much of its original meaning, and, in a comprehensive sense, signifies skill employed to accomplish an end. According to the end, there are the subdivisions into mechanical and liberal. If the *mechanical* arts do not aim beyond producing an impression upon matter, the *liberal* aspire to produce an impression upon man.

Whatever the end in view, the bond which unites the spectator and the work is *interest* (*inter*, between; *esse*, to be; that which is between). This bond gives the first condition necessary to success. Art may be classified according to the character of the impression it produces. If the impression is elevating, it is *fine* art. Impressions which neither elevate nor lower belong to *mixed* art. Impressions which lower are the result of *debased* art. The highest aim of fine art is not found short of the perfection of all things.

What are the *means* available?

Our better and worse qualities are equally susceptible of growth, and the exercise of a faculty is known to strengthen and develop it. Whatever brings into play our higher nature, develops it, and is, therefore, elevating in its influence; and the *fine arts are addressed to the higher nature of man*. The embodiment of this address is the work of art, and the *work of fine art is an embodiment of elevating thoughts and feelings*.

Inspiration excepted, there is no obvious way of reaching the thoughts and feelings of others, but by an impression conveyed through the senses. Then *art implies an impression conveyed through the senses*. Hence deprecation of sensuous means is vain, unless these means convey no feeling or thought that is elevating.

If art implies skill, then one of the first rules must be, *not to endeavor to express through one art what may be more readily expressed through another*. This somewhat neglected rule leads to the inquiry into the capabilities of different means of expression : *Poetry*, by means of language ; *Music*, through sound ; *Painting*, through form and color ; *Sculpture*, by solid matter itself; *Architecture*, by combinations of several of these; *Dancing*, by movement—are each adapted to express certain classes of things better than others, and it is a good practice not to select for painting a subject which sculpture will better express, and not to paint in words what may be more effectively

MODES OF EXPRESSION.   147

painted in colors. Certain *modes of expression* are common, but in a different degree, to these arts. *Transposition* and *generalization* are of much use. Thus the *Metaphor* (to carry over), which transfers the figure of one object to another; the *Emblem* (to throw in), which represents the whole object by a connected part; the *Symbol* (to throw with), which represents a quality by some object which includes or possesses eminently that quality, or which represents an idea by a sign; the *Hyperbole* (to throw over), which explains by intentional exaggeration; the *History* (to know), which recites events known or believed to be real; the *Fiction*, which recites imagined events; the *Parable* (to throw beside), which recites a supposed history thrown beside a corresponding real history in order to draw a moral; the *Allegory* (other speech), which describes a sequence of things intangible by the image of tangible things—are all available elements.

Imitation is a great resource in the arts.

Imitation which reproduces similarity by means of a complete reproduction *of the totality of objects*, belongs to the mechanical or manufacturing arts.

Imitation in the fine arts is *intentionally incomplete;* natural objects are not here reproduced by their totality, but by their image; and this image represents the complete ideal of the object, not the object itself in all its parts. This rule bears with particular force upon details. The most effective stage of a work is clearly the proper one at which to arrest it; and this is *the stage of greatest suggestion* or greatest promise. As Lessing remarks: " If the artist can never avail himself of more than a single moment of ever-changing Nature, and that from a single point of view . . . . this moment should be *the moment of greatest promise, not of greatest fulfillment*, for the imagination of the spectator must have free play." The value of incomplete imitation is seen here.

What are the best subjects for imitation? The contemplation of *perfection* is felt to be elevating. Things partly imperfect produce varied emotions; each part intensifies by contrast the character of the other, and a ready way of rendering perfection sensible is to place it in contrast with imperfection. This may be done in different manners. Thus the spectacle of a hero possessing some of our foibles and certain virtues, reminding us of what high traits we may hope to acquire, may be presented so as to interest and elevate; or the same subject may be presented in a manner to confuse and render evil attractive, and to lower us. In the influence of a work we find a limit to the representation of *the imperfect*, as well as of every other element in art.

The *type*, or impressed form; the *ideal type*, or form impressed with the idea; the *chimerical*, or form capable of no existence, except in thought; the *picturesque*, or formed like a picture; the *grotesque*, or wildly formed; the *deformed;* the *ironical*, which seemingly approves yet disapproves; the *satirical*, which keenly exposes to mingled laughter and contempt; the *sarcastic*, in which laughter slackens and contempt is intensified; the *comic*, which deals with life in its light and amusing phases; the *burlesque*, which amuses by exaggeration; *buffoonery*, by puffing of cheeks and low pleasantries; *tragedy*, which treats of pain and terror, and strikes the spectator with compassion and fear—in a word, the *dramatic*, which includes the other elements, and presents life in all its phases, perfect and imperfect, sublime, familiar, and trivial, is a legitimate element in art, according to its influence. In the same way historical and religious subjects are included, for moral beauty and dramatic interest attach to them.

In certain Greek tragedies innocence and beauty were made to succumb to crime. This form of art was condemned by Socrates and Plato, but upheld by Aristotle. If the spectacle of down-trodden virtue was so presented as to chasten the spectator by sympathetic suffering, then its introduction was legitimate.

In choosing between different elements, we may remember that form is nearer the essence of things than color, for the destruction of an object can hardly be effected without destroying

CONVERGENCE OF EFFECTS. 149

its form, but its color frequently remains unaltered; that much of the pleasure due to the contemplation of beauty results from *a pleasing train of progressing thought*, developing new ideas and sensations on the way; that *addressing the imagination* is a chief means in art; that the imagination to be pleased must have free play; that the mere beauty of matter is small compared to the beauty with which it may be invested by *expression ;* that means have value according to their *power of expression ;* that matter and most things owe much of their expression to *association ;* that association is a source of power; that power exerted in one direction is *cumulative* in its effect, hence the need of *unity* and the advantage attending *convergence of effects ;* that the focus of convergence is the *unit* embodied in the work; that a work is permanent in interest according to the permanent value of the unit it embodies; that the most elementary truth, being the broadest in its application, is the most permanent in interest; that truth is attractive according to its influence; that beauty is attractive according to its perfection; that the most beautiful and elementary work of all is a suggestion or glorification, in some shape, of the truth, beauty, and perfection of the All-pervading Unity.

Since the expression of the beautiful is a chief means in art, it is of interest to ascertain its nature. There is the fine definition of Plato, "*Beauty is the splendor of truth.*" If we could rest there, all would be simple. But certain ancients defined it variously, as the *expression of the invisible, the expression of the moral ideal, the expression of human passion.* Coleridge confuses us by calling it *multitude in unity ;* and Wordsworth clears the paradox by explaining it as *a multiplicity of symmetrical parts uniting in a consistent whole.* Greenough defines beauty as *the promise of function*, a definition in which there is more promise than function. Torrey calls it the *truth of eternal relations.* Taine gives no definition in his " Philosophie de l'Art," but remarks to his pupils that he knows two precepts: " The first, which counsels to be born with genius—it is the affair of your parents, not mine; the second, which counsels to work much in order to possess well one's art—it is your affair, again it is not mine." Locke defines beauty as *a composition causing delight;* another, as *the perfection of its kind expressed by its chief characteristics;* Webster, as *an assemblage of properties which pleases;* while Owen Jones remarks that *true beauty results from the repose which the mind feels when the eye, the intellect, and the affections, are satisfied from the absence of any want.* This instructive and practical definition, by a great student of ornament, is in a fair way to be established as a maxim in decorative art, yet it is deficient. If the farthest aim of the artist is to produce *repose*, what is to incite him to action? The *Tao* of the Chinese and the *Nirwana* of the Buddhists is, according to the conception of some, a state of repose; and this conception of happiness is called annihilation. The most imperative want of living beings is action, the triple action of Demosthenes, the "Viva, viva, viva" of the Perugian motto. Since action is an imperative want, the absence of any want implies action, which is, of course, incompatible with repose; so the terms of this definition of Owen Jones are contradictory.

Perhaps when we say, *The beautiful is the expression of perfection*, we approach in some measure to a definition that may be of practical use. Whatever of beauty resides in an object seems to be the expression of some perfection, and no object appears in any degree beautiful that does not possess some perfection. Physical beauty is the expression of some physical perfection, as a beautiful countenance is the expression of some moral perfection.

The nature of grace may be suggested. If *grace is the expression of the sense of measure*, then it implies the perception of truth and of relation. The perception of truth being obscured by the imperfections of our nature, and exalted by perfection, a high degree of grace implies a superiority of nature, which leads to perfect self-command under severe trials. Want of grace, however, does not exclude high character; it merely indicates incompleteness or a want of the sense of measure.

The impression of the *sublime* has been attributed to various causes (from the Latin *superum*, of the gods; *limen*, door—*at the door of the gods*). Burke refers it to fear and the *instinct of self-preservation;* Ruskin, to the *effect of greatness* on our feelings; Allston, to *a sense of infinite harmony;* Boileau, to "a certain form of speech, proper to elevate and ravish the soul, which comes either from the magnitude of the thought, the loftiness of the feeling, or the magnificence of language, or the harmonious, animated, and lively turn of thought." It appears to me that, to be impressed with the feeling of the sublime, it is sufficient that a thing should *pass our capacity to measure*. The sublime would then be *the expression of the immeasurable*. If this is a true view, then the sublime can never be *fully expressed* in art: the utmost that art can do is to *suggest* it; in this respect it differs from beauty, which, being finite, is at least susceptible to that extent of complete expression; we have seen, however, that the moment of greatest suggestion is sufficient in art. The indication of a line without end, a plain without limit, enhances the effect of numerous compositions, in a manner which few stop to analyze. Similarly, there is something sublime in certain things undefined, such as light undefined; and we observe that it is beyond our capacity to measure.

The ordinary objects which surround us daily influence our happiness more than is realized by those who rest content with the too frequent ugliness of modern life. *Ugly* is from the old English *ugsome*, frightful; the Anglo-Saxon *egle*, hateful; the Gothic *agls*, base, and *ogjan*, to frighten; and the Icelandic *ôgn*, terror; and the word is here used in its modern sense, added to that of its antecedents. We doubtless desire to be surrounded by beautiful objects, but this cannot be attained until the industrial arts are dignified by union with the liberal arts, the artist and artisan united in one person, and beauty and fitness are found together.

In this direction England and France have lately made progress, and America will not remain behind in the generous race.

PROPOSITIONS IN ORNAMENT.

The study of decorative art suggests the following propositions:

1. To express beauty and grace is the first aim of ornament.
2. Ornamentation consists in imitations of natural objects idealized, or of the significant parts of natural objects selected and combined: the selections must be suitable to the materials, implements, and process to be used, and to the objects to be ornamented.
3. Minute details are usually more curious than beautiful, and those tending to divert attention from the important characteristics of the work should be omitted.
4. Unity and harmonious balance of all the parts of a composition, namely, of expression, form, color, and texture, are indispensable to beauty and grace.
5. Variety under proper limits, in the subordinate parts, serves to enliven the effect and avoid monotony.
6. Order and symmetry of the principal parts, and great magnitude expressed in a large or small space, are conducive to grandeur.
7. Imitations of the beautiful in Nature, in strict conformity with the laws of Nature, constitute perfect ornament.

In the application of these propositions certain corollaries follow:

Thus, harmonious composition of line, including tangential, flowing, radiating, and geometrical lines; harmonious distribution of form; contrast, distribution, and balance of light and shade; and contrast, distribution, and balance of color, the effect of texture, should be studied and applied.

Sometimes, in Nature, variety invades the principal parts, but it will be observed that a certain balance is still maintained in the whole; this may be followed by the artist, but the greater the variety introduced, the greater will be the skill required to maintain the balance of the whole.

Ornamental objects may be divided into two parts: the frame, and the subject framed. The framework admits of less variety, and should be treated in a style simple and severe, according to its function. The subject admits of greater variety, limited by the principle of unity. The background between the subject and framework should be intermediate in treatment, and place the subject in medium relief.

The relations between an ornamental object and its surroundings are to be kept in view. Thus, in the walls of a room, the whole space decorated forms the background to its ornaments, and its prevailing color should have reference to a proper relief of such ornaments; also, to persons or objects for the use of which the room is intended.

Decoration may not inaptly be compared to a tree, the roots of which are supplied by the knowledge and feeling of the artist: the branches are the framework, the leaves the background; the flowers are the various subjects, and the fruit, if it bear any, is in its æsthetic and moral effect. Similarly in Oriental ornament we see subjects distributed over a surface, somewhat like flowers on a bush (*see* Fig. 44).

In general, much benefit may be derived by the study of existing styles of ornament, and of their success in interpreting Nature (*see* Fig. 45).

The great influence of surrounding objects on the mind gives importance to the principles of decoration. The grave and depressing effects of sombre colors, gloomy lights, lowering clouds, and leafless trees, are familiar to all. Equally so are the cheering influences of lively or even mild and soft colors, of sunlight and fleecy clouds, of spring-like foliage; and walls tinted in blue or violet are said to cure certain forms of mental derangement.

The *mise en scène* of a subject chosen for decoration should be selected and arranged so as to express the period, the spot, the time, the accidents of light and shade, the architectural effect, the disposition of the ground, the atmospheric circumstances, which, as a well-chosen framework, bring out in proper relief the idea or event represented.

Flatness, now so much advocated, often runs to excess. The Pompeians, who decorated effectively, shaded their ornaments enough to give distinctness and accentuate the forms, but not enough to detach it from the ground, or to produce too much relief. This limit may also be safely applied to ornament in the round.

The preceding propositions are applicable to architectural ornament, to works in metal, stone, wood, textiles, glass, and pottery. They are exemplified in majolica. Unity, and fitness of ornament to the subject, are usually seen. Thus, toilet-basins were adorned with aquatic allegories, fruit-stands with fruits and vintage-scenes, wine-cups with festoons of vine, religious pieces with Christian symbols, *amatoria* (love-tokens) with hearts and Cupids, *credenze* (services) with the owner's arms, *albarelli* (drug-vessels) with decorative labels, *piatti da pompa* (show-plates) with a variety of becoming designs. The subdivision of each object into two parts, the subject and the framework, is usually seen. The borders of plates and dishes, the bands around the top and bottom of vases, are treated with balanced floral forms and sprays of leaves, severe in treatment compared to the free play of line of the subjects in the centre. The ornament was well distributed, and specially designed for the spaces it had to fill.

A conventional treatment was universally adopted, and more severe in the best periods. The composition of line, especially in the folds of drapery in the early period, recalls the breadth of good mosaic or Florentine medals, as in the

Faustina dish (Fig. 32), or in the plate inscribed ORATIO P. (Fig. 29).

The intermediate decorative treatment of the backgrounds, where inscribed scrolls or Persian floral figures are loosely scattered, is also met with in the backgrounds of pre-Raphaelite paintings.

The introduction of *grotesques* in decoration springs from the love of the marvelous, and pleases the imagination. In ornament, more even than in painting or sculpture, every subject requires to be idealized, and the introduction of chimerical beings embodying certain attributes is a language entirely legitimate. The figures usually called grotesques are more properly *chimerical*. The real grotesque is also found in decoration, and the propriety of its introduction has been questioned. If all must be idealized, how can we idealize ugliness and deformity? The *true grotesque* is a comic element : it is not gay ; it touches laughter, compassion, and disdain. Hilarity is associated with pity, and laughter with tears.

If art resides not in the beautiful alone, but in the contrast of beauty and ugliness, of greatness and triviality, as sometimes seen in Nature, then the grotesque is admissible. The chimerical, which presents creations capable of existence only in thought, and does not imply ugliness, may also be introduced.

When the car of Thespis amused the Athenians, with bedaubed faces and cloven-footed human divinities, it was an instance of the chimerical and grotesque united.

Morto da Feltro and *Giovanni da Udine* set the grotesques in fashion ; they were assisted by *Mariotto* and *Raffaelo Metidoro*. *Bachiacca, Baldasare*, and *Peruzzi*, of Siena, became celebrated in this line ; while Prospero Œsi was called *Prospero dalle Grottesche*. *Pier di Cosimo, Mecherino, Razzi, Cristoforo Rustici, Giorgio da Siena*, and *Lomazzo*, became known in this specialty.

The impression that Raphael (Raffaele Sanzio) designed for majolica appears to rest on uncertain evidence. It is stated that his father, a painter of ordinary merit, employed him in painting fayence before his apprenticeship to Perugino, which began in his twelfth year. Don Vittorio, in his *Osservazione sopra Felsina Pittrice*, alludes to a letter from Raffaele referring to majolica designs, and supplied by him to a duchess (*see* J. Dennistoun). However this may be, no majolica known to be his remains; and the so-called Raphael ware consists in part of ornamentation in the style of Raphael, and partly of copies from pictures, or from engravings of pictures, painted by him. Neither are these to be confounded with the productions of Raffaele del Colle (Raffaelino), a painter of some power, who, according to Taja, was employed by Raphael on the History of Moses in Horeb; also in the Farnesina, and also by Giulio in the Hall of Constantine. He also decorated the "Imperiale" Palace at Pesaro, and prepared majolica designs for Guidobaldo I. Nor are they to be confounded with the works of Raffaele Ciarla, a potter, and pupil of Orazio Fontana (1530–1560); nor with those of Raffaele Girolamo, at Monte Lupo, in 1639.

RAPHAELESQUE DECORATION.

Pietro Perugino was the first to reproduce the painted grotesque ancient Roman decoration. His pupil, *Raphael*, did not decorate the Loggie of the Vatican until after he had worked at the Sala di Cambio and the Library at Siena. He is criticised in this instance for want of proportion between the size of the scrolls and the flowers and figures, want of symmetry, and for mixing symbols of mythology and Christianity together. In his later work, the decoration of the Villa Madama, for which he made the first designs, he avoided these points; there is more proportion and symmetry, more repose and unity.

Although the *Baths of Titus* present the models from which originated this decoration, the Raphaelesque style was more copious and profuse. Clusters of fruit in regular masses, cassoons, and archivolts, not seen in the Roman baths, were introduced, and less use was made of primary colors. The variety of tone and forms in the Loggia is of more difficult treatment, but when skillfully disposed produces superior effects. It is at once the highest, most spiritual, and most difficult style of decorative ornament yet developed. It is perhaps inferior in distribution to Oriental ornament, but this defect is not inherent in the style itself. Being the most difficult, it has, in the hands of the uneducated, degenerated into a multitude of pastry-like scrolls and cartouches, which surfeit the eye, and are misnamed Renaissance. *Giulio Romano*, while associated with Raphael, worked in good taste; but later he fell into extravagance and caricature.

A similar degeneracy is seen in the Louis XV. style, in which straight lines, ovals, squares, and circles, are avoided, and a lax S-curve predominates. It may be said of this school, as Pierre Guérin said of Camucini: "He nourished himself upon the ancients and Raphael, but never knew how to digest them."

In the sixteenth century the paintings in the Baths of Titus were faint and almost obliterated; but the books of Vitruvius had been found. This author, like Pliny, judged harshly of the Roman and Pompeian decoration, but his censure sounds like praise. "Every one," says Vitruvius, "who has seen these extravagances, far from denouncing them, is invariably pleased with them."

The critic Hittorf remarks of the Loggia that "the first effect is that of a picture repeated one thousand-fold, glittering in beautiful colors and forms, filling us with confused and excited sensations; these emotions gradually becoming subdued, until the eye is able to seize every individual subject, analyze it, and admire without ceasing. Richness of resource has reached a climax."

HINTS FOR PAINTING ON POTTERY.

VITRIFIABLE colors are obtainable ground in powder, or put up in tubes mixed with fat oil of turpentine.

Vitrifiable colors consist of two parts: the coloring matter, and the vitreous matter. The *coloring matter* consists of one or several metals, metallic oxides, or metallic salts. The *vitreous matter* is also called *flux*, and consists usually of sand, borax, and oxide of lead. The colors may be classed, according to the temperature required to fuse them, as follows:

1. *Ordinary soft muffle-colors* (*couleurs de moufle tendres*).—These melt at about 800° centigrade, or low cherry-heat.

2. *Hard muffle-colors* (*couleurs de moufle dures*).—These present the advantage of not being altered, when, after a first firing at about 1000° C. (fusion of silver), they are painted upon with the softer ordinary muffle-colors, or gilt.

3. *Hard-fire colors* (*couleurs de grand feu*).—These fuse at a white heat, such as that in the kilns where hard porcelain is glazed, or about 1,500° C.

Firing of the Colors.—The firing is best done by *china decorators*, whose addresses are seen in the directories of the principal cities. The painted piece should be dried slowly, and protected from dust and moisture. It is well to require the muffle to be dry, and free from noxious vapors. I mention here Mr. George Warrin, 155 West Broadway, New York, who has often fired decorative tile-work for me, and to my entire satisfaction. Other decorators are Messrs. Bennett & White, and Mr. Edward Lycett. Addresses where colors may be procured are given in the chapter on Modern Fayence.

Hard-Fire Decoration-Painting.—Two methods are used. In the first, the body of the ware after one firing, which brings it to the state of *biscuit*, is dipped in a liquid stanniferous enamel, which adheres by absorption to the surface; this is allowed to dry; the outlines are then stenciled or traced upon the pulverulent surface, and the vitrifiable hard-fire colors are then applied, as in *fresco*, with decision, and require to be correctly laid at the first stroke, as touching up is almost impossible on the powdered surface, which is also soluble in water. The piece is then fired in a kiln, the colors and enamel fuse together, and a certain softness and brilliancy is the result.

A similar process is used in *under-the-glaze painting* upon white earthenware and terra-cotta. After painting and heating sufficiently to expel any fat-substance that may have been used with the colors, the piece is dipped in a liquid glaze, usually plumbeous, dried, and fired. This method offers the advantage of brilliancy of tone and glaze, although the range of colors is more limited than with softer muffle-colors. It is usual to render the ground less absorbent before applying the colors, by dipping it in water, or by coating it with a solution of gum, sugar, milk, albumen, or spirits of turpentine. The vehicle used for the colors may be aqueous or fat, separately or in succession. There is some advantage in tracing the outlines, for instance, with a fat-pigment, and washing in the tints with an aqueous pigment, for the latter will not then disturb the outlines.

The process requires the same certainty as *fresco* decoration. As the ware is so absorbent that the colors sink in rapidly and change their appearance, it is well to have alongside a piece of glazed china, upon which each tone is laid to judge of its value.

In the second, the biscuit body coated with the enamel is fired, and upon the white, glossy, hard enamel surface the painting is done with hard-fire colors. Touching up and alterations are easily effected, and a third firing fuses the colors and enamel, with much the same brilliancy as in the first method.

The hard-fire colors are few; they are chiefly violet or manganese brown, brown, green, yellow, ochre, and blue. Red is almost unobtainable. A pink is obtained from chromium and tin; the ordinary greens are from copper, while turquoise-green is from copper and soda.

Painting in Muffle-Colors.—This is done over the fired enamel or glaze with colors that fuse at a lower temperature, which can be properly attained in muffles. The range of tone of these colors is more extended; red made from gold, carmine, purple of Cassius, and other soft colors, distinguish this process. Most of these colors have the same tone before and after firing. At Florence this process is taught at an academy. The possession of a complete series of vitrifiable colors that will not alter in tone by firing is still a great desideratum for the artist. The presence of lead or tin in the glaze is a potent cause of alteration. The glaze of hard porcelain is feldspathic and contains no lead, and the hard-fire colors applied to it are not altered.

A fixed white (*blanc fixe, bianco fisso*) and a white for mixing, or Chinese white (*blanc à mêler*), serve for much the same use as white-lead does in ordinary oil-painting.

Mixing of Colors.—Colors of one manufacture will not always mix well with those of another; it is therefore better to use only those of one maker in mixtures.

Colors containing *iron* (they are red, flesh-red, brown-red, violet of iron, browns, yellow-browns, ochres, blacks, and grays, excepting platinum-gray) do not mix well with *cobalt* blues, as iron and cobalt fired together produce a gray varying from light to black. Colors containing iron, when mixed with yellows, alter them when made of other metals, such as antimony, but mix well with yellows made from iron.

Colors containing *gold* (purple of Cassius, carmine, mauve, ruby, carmine lake, pink, violet of gold) are not easily fired. A low heat leaves them yellowish and dull, a too high heat turns them dark and purplish; nor do they mix well with colors containing iron. Much lead also tarnishes them.

PAINTING IN MUFFLE-COLORS. 161

Coral-red made from chromate of lead is unstable, and does not mix well. All other colors may be mixed. Ivory-yellow is very fusible, and devours or dissolves colors over which it is laid; applied thinly, however, it increases their gloss; it mixes well with flesh-red for flesh-tints. Silver-yellow and yellow ochre, with greens and blue-greens, produce numerous greens. Copper-green is usually brighter (but sometimes turns dark) than chrome-green, which is more permanent. Browns will shade almost all colors. A sample of all the colors, alone or mixed, should be kept before the eyes in painting.

To prepare a Color.—To the color in powder add its volume of fat-essence, and incorporate it by means of the palette-knife. In the colors in tubes this has been already done.

Outlines.—These may be stenciled, or the lines may be traced with black lithographic crayon directly on the glaze; or the glazed surface may be coated with turpentine-spirits, and, when dry, drawn upon with a lead-pencil. An outline that disappears in firing may be traced with ordinary India-ink.

To trace the outline in color, mix the color with lavender-oil, and draw the lines with a steel or quill pen, or brush. This outline should be with fat-color, in a narrow line.

To lay in the first wash of color, to the color add spirits of turpentine (lavender has the advantage of drying slowly), and with a large brush apply in parallel strokes rapidly, without minuteness. Always fill the brush to the same extent.

The facility of *working over previous work* depends upon a careful use of essences. Fixed strokes are made by using less fat-essence. Strokes that present lighter and darker parts at once may be made by adding more turpentine-spirits. Deep colors are not obtained by using much fat-oil (this would spoil in firing), but by repeated washes lightly superposed, and using more spirits. High lights may be taken out with a brush or rag, or reserved. In general, the light colors are first laid, and worked over with the darker ones. No brilliancy should remain on the surface of a color when it is touched again with a somewhat dry color, otherwise it will be dissolved and disturbed.

After the first firing, if the contrast of colors is unsatisfactory, the work may be corrected, using little fat-oil, and not too much color. Sometimes additional firings are resorted to. Each firing should be at a lower heat than the previous. For many purposes one firing is sufficient.

To produce delicate shading, for *carmine* use a gray made of carmine No. 2 and blue-green, also with yellow for mixing (*jaune à mêler*). *Blues* may be shaded by Victoria blue, by carmine, and by violet of iron. For *yellows*, use in succession yellows for mixing, deep yellow, and ochre; or else with a gray made of deep or silver yellow, with a little purple or gold violet, and less of blue-green; red marks on yellow ground must be reserved, unless the yellow is an iron-yellow. For *reds* for the lights, use flesh-red, and shade successively with capucin-red, deep red, violet of iron, and red-gray. *Greens* are made of blue-green mixed with light and deep yellow; of gray-green, with light blue. Chrome and emerald green and ochres are first laid in flat tints, and worked over with a gray formed of chrome-green, ochre, and yellow. The deeper touches are of emerald-green with ochre and brown (108).

For flesh, mix equal flesh-red and ivory-yellow; apply flat. Carnations are made with flesh-red alone, used fat; shade with iron-violet hatchings. Shadows cast on flesh are made with gray-black. Linen is shaded with gray-black, to which dark blue is added. For brown hair, use brown 108 with some blue, and shade with brown 108 alone. When two colors are superposed, the most fusible should be placed underneath. In general, the irregularity of the strokes may be used so as greatly to enhance the forms.

Unevenness of surface may be removed by rubbing with sand-paper. Before firing, any desired part may be scraped away, or dissolved in spirits of turpentine and removed. After firing, any part painted over the glaze may be removed by dissolving in fluorhydric acid, which is powerful, and difficult of use.

MISCELLANEOUS NOTES.

AMONG the Italian names of elements of ornamentation are: *Trofei*, trophies; *cerquate*, oak-branches; *foglie*, leaves; *foglie da dozzena*, leaves by the dozen; *paesi*, landscapes; *tirate*, interlacing on white ground; *porcellana*, scrolls and flowers on white resembling blue and white porcelain decoration; *sopra bianco*, on white ground; *groppi*, groups; *con fondi* and *senza*, with a ground and without; *frutti*, fruits; *a quartiere*, decorated in radiating compartments; *fiori*, flowers and birds; *rabesche*, arabesques; *grotesche*, grotesques; *candellieri*, chandelier); symmetrical scrolls or grotesques (*see* Castel Durante).

Among the SYMBOLS and EMBLEMS are: the glory, aureole, and nimbus; the fish, emblem of water and the rite of baptism; the cross, the lamb, the lion; the dragon, for sin and paganism; the hind, the unicorn, of chastity; the dove, the emblem of the soul, of purity, and of the Holy Ghost; the olive, of peace; the palm, of martyrs; the lily, of purity and chastity; the fruit, of the fruit of the Spirit; the taper, of piety; the fire and flames, of zeal and fervor; the flaming heart, of fervent piety and spiritual love; the crown, when on the Madonna, for the Regina Angelorum; on a martyr, it means victory over sin; also, a bride, or Bride of Christ; the sword, axe, lance, and club, indicate the manner of martyrdom; the banner, of victory; the chalice, of faith; the Book, the Testament, Scriptures, or sign of learning; the ship, of the Christian Church; the anchor, of hope; ears of corn and bunches of grapes, of the bread and wine of the Eucharist; the candelabrum, of Christ; the sponge, nails, the five wounds, and many other figures, of the Passion and Crucifixion.

White is worn by the Saviour after his resurrection, and signified purity, chastity, and light; ruby-red, divine love; heat, the creative power; sapphire-blue signified truth and fidelity; emerald-green, hope, victory, and spring; yellow or gold, the sun, goodness, and marriage and fruitfulness; violet or amethyst, suffering, penitence; gray, penance and humility; black, humility and mourning, also darkness and wickedness, and death. These were general symbols; the particular symbols are too numerous to be given here. (*See* "Handbook," by Mrs. C. E. Clement.)

The symbols of angels form an interesting object of study. Dionysius divides them into councilors, rulers, and messengers of God. The councilors were: first, and nearest to God, the seraphim, from the Hebrew *saraph*, to burn, to be eminent, representing love; and second, the cherubim, from the Hebrew *kerab*, to grasp, representing knowledge. These two ever stand before God, adoring and praising him; while the thrones support his throne. The rulers, which regulate the universe, were: dominations, with a sword; virtues, in armor, with an axe and pennon; powers, with a *bâton*. The messengers, in armor, with pennons or lily, were subdivided into archangels and angels, which, in Greek, signified *a bringer of tidings*. The early masters treated the seraphs in red, to represent love, and the cherubs in blue, for knowledge; and their positions signified that love is nearer to divine nature than wisdom. The seraphs were covered with eyes. The cherubim had six wings. The wings found in Egypt, Phœnicia, and Persia, signified the flight of time; also, the flight of spirit. The Persians had a complete theory of angels—twelve angels for the twelve months, thirty for the thirty days of the month, and an angel for each day in the year; they had angels of light and angels of darkness, and contests of angels, and the names of their angels have passed into Christianity. The Persian word

NAMES OF ITALIAN PIECES TRANSLATED. 165

mage has given us image and imagination; a *mage* is a priest—one who deals with the spirit or essence of things, as does imagination in art.

Among the designations of Italian pieces are: *Piatti da pompa*, dishes intended for decoration, or show-plates, usually over fifteen inches diameter, with two holes pierced in the circular projection on the back to receive a cord, by which they are suspended; *bacini*, or *bacili*, shallow basins, or saucer-shaped plates; *mesciroba*, ewer; *brocca*, pitcher, water-pot; *mezzina*, jug, or pitcher; *chicchere*, coffee-cup; *chicchere de farmacia*, vessels for apothecaries; *albarello*, drug-pot; *ongaresca*, or *piadena*, a cup mounted on a stem; *fiaschini*, flat bottle, or pilgrim-flask; *bacinette*, deep saucer for amatoria; *fruttiere*, fruit-dish; *saliera*, salt-cellar; *vasi gamelii*, or *nuziali*, marriage services; *scodella*, a peculiar basin on a foot; *tondino*, a peculiar form of plate, with a deep centre and wide, flat brim; *presentatoio*, a flat, circular plate, on which to present a glass of wine; *amatoria*, love-gifts, presented full of fruit or sweetmeats, somewhat as a *bonbonnière*; *tagliere*, plate; *credenze*, services, and services for presents; *credenza*, high-backed sideboard; *boccale*, decanter; *boccaletto*, small pitcher; *tazza*, raised cup; *coppa*, cup; *scrivania*, inkstand; *profumiera*, perfuming-pan; *profumiere*, perfumer; *canestrella*, basket-like pieces; *smartellati*, saucers moulded with *repoussé* panels and ornaments; *dozzinale*, common pieces, or by the dozen; *vasi puerperali*, or *scudella da donna di parto*, are sets of five or seven pieces, fitting together in the shape of a vase, for the use of ladies in confinement, consisting of a scodella, tagliere, ongaresca, saliera, and cover; the *tazza*, or *coppa di partoriente*, had a similar use.

In the sixteenth century, the ordinary prices paid to painters for borders, etc., were as follows per hundred plates, giving to the ducal crown its absolute value of $1.02, or four shillings, threepence, one farthing: For trophies, one crown; arabesques, sixty-eight cents; cerquati, fifty cents; grotesques in white cameo on blue ground, $2.04; grotesques in style of

Venice, $2.72; leaves, $1.02; flowers and fruit, thirty-four cents.

Allowing even twelve times the absolute value as the proper relative value (*see* J. Dennistoun), these prices seem very small, even when it is considered that the borders were usually painted by less expert hands than the central subjects.

The currency of the duchy of Urbino, in the sixteenth century, was as follows in absolute value: One ducal crown, or two-thirds of a Roman crown, $1.02 gold; one florin, or two-thirds of a ducal crown, sixty-eight cents; one lira, or one-third of a ducal crown, thirty-four cents; one paul, about ten cents; the gros was one-third of a paul; the bolognino was one-third of a gros.

MODERN FAYENCE AT THE EXHIBITION OF 1876.

FRANCE.

FAÏENCERIE OF GIEN, Loiret, France. This manufactory is noted for its ordinary fayence, and that in the old French style. Their printed decoration in colors on vases presents colors of great brilliancy, and a glossy glaze containing lead and borax. Some of the decoration is in relief, with a white paste, which is afterward colored on the surface under the glaze. E PETIT and A. MARROIS paint pretty landscapes. The reviva of the Rouen decoration has a certain interest, and the cheapness of the printed reproductions in the Italian style places them in the reach of all.

A. MONTAGNON, of Nevers, France, shows some artistic fayence, chiefly painted in blue and yellow. Some of the outlines are good, and the variety of forms and originality of the hand-painted subjects are praiseworthy. Some of the vases are in the Rouen style; others are Moresque and Persian in sentiment.

HAVILAND & Co., of Limoges, France, have made technical progress in colors and glazes for fayence; also for porcelain. They have succeeded in obtaining transparent enamel colors in relief upon the glaze of hard porcelain, as the Japanese and Chinese frequently do. This result has been long sought for in Europe, and constitutes an important progress. Soft French porcelain is also one of their products, and a new palette of colors for fayence, which, after firing, assume a highly vitreous appearance, is noticeable. Some of their fayence hand-painted tiles have been ordered by M. Garnier for panels in the smoking-room of the New Opera, in Paris. TONY NOËL and DELAPLANCHE, sculptors; PALLANDRE, flower-painter; BRACQUEMOND, etcher of copperplates used in chromo-lithography, are to be mentioned here also. P. HUSSON, chemist, who, in aiming at the qualities of Deck's work, obtained other valuable results, and CHAPLET, LINDENCHER, and LAFON, may be mentioned among the artists.

J. AUBRY, Bellevue, near Toul, makes pottery in the Faenza style—that is, of terra-cotta, coated with a stanniferous enamel. Some of the decoration is in the style of Rouen, Marseilles, Moustier, etc. The drawing is frequently bold.

BARBIZET & SON, Paris, produce good modeled work in the Palissy style, of a white body, coated with a thin, soft, lead glaze, often crackled.

TH. SERGENT, Paris, deserves mention among producers of economical artistic fayence, and for a bust of Diana of Poitiers.

EUGÈNE BLOT, of Boulogne-sur-Mer, gives admirable lifelike expression to the unglazed terra-cotta statuettes modeled by him. The subjects relate chiefly to fishermen and sea-side life.

JULES HOURY, Paris, makes fayence plaques for furniture.

A. DUSSON signs modern pieces of most brilliant enamel colors.

A. HACHE & P. LEHALLEUR, Paris and Vierzon, deserve mention here as having succeeded in making admirably thin porcelain cups, equaling, in that respect, the Oriental, and of a brilliant, creamy white. The paste is cast liquid into a plaster mould. Sometimes it is ribbed.

The work of DECK, COLLINOT, and PARVILLÉE, has been spoken of in the Persian group.

P. E. VAQUEREL, 27 Rue des Petits Hôtels, Paris, prepares sheets printed in vitrifiable colors, which may be transferred to earthenware or porcelain, and fixed permanently by firing.

This process, improperly called *decalcomania*, is, like chromolithography, susceptible of doing excellent service with proper designs and within certain limits. The designs are mostly ill-suited to the process. Mr. C. Moller, 35 Maiden Lane, is the agent in New York.

ENGLAND.

A. B. DANIELL & SON, London, supply admirable pieces from the Worcester Royal Porcelain Works, from Minton's, and from Rose & Co., Coalbrookdale. Some features of this ware deserve particular notice. At Worcester: the under-glaze painting on bony porcelain, producing soft effects; the " gold-aventurine," turquoise-beaded " trembleuse cup," the reproductions of old Worcester, expressly executed for Messrs. Daniell from models lent by them; the "inlaid-clay " work, executed under the glaze in an ivory body; Florentine nautilus cups, reproductions of Japanese; pieces inclosed in perforated work; subjects painted in white enamel on cobalt-blue ground, in the style of Limoges enamel; arabesques in the sixteenth-century style, designed by Mr. Bott, all highly finished and costly, from Minton's; gold in relief, mat-gold etching, porcelain decorated in imitation of Canton cloisonné enamels, made through the initiative of Messrs. Daniell; admirable Cupids in pink monochrome; Solon's unrivaled *pâte-sur-pâte*, and charming conceptions; new "inlaid-clay " subjects; C. Toft's work, Henry II. reproductions. In earthenware: Mussill's under-glaze opaque enamel colored subjects, of brilliant effect; so-called " majolica " in a variety of styles, less harmonious than the Italian type. At Coalbrookdale: The rich Cashmere services made from designs supplied by Messrs. Daniell; pilgrim bottles, of dark-blue ground, with gold design, presenting a bloomy effect, may be mentioned as of special interest; also, disks of buff clay, painted under the glaze by H. S. Marks, and a plaque called " The Listener," painted on fayence over the glaze.

GIBBS & MOORE, London, show panels of hand-painted tiles; some, in monochrome, particularly successful.

T. C. Brown, Westhead, Moore & Co., Staffordshire, make earthenware with a new series of printed designs of natural-history subjects, treated with spirit by Mr. Brown, of London; plateaux by W. P. Rhodes, painted in brown outlines and flat tints, with flesh shadows hatched in blue-gray, opaque white for high lights, and a favorite turquoise sky; also printed tiles.

Watcombe Terra-Cotta Company, Torquay, are fortunate in possessing an admirable red clay, and cast it liquid, or model it into delicately-formed figures.

W. Brownfield & Son, Cobridge, Staffordshire, show good work from the artists L. H. Jahn, Sandier, Rouse, Cartledge.

Campbell Brick and Tile Company, Stoke-on-Trent, present some good mural tiles, printed.

R. Minton Taylor, Stoke-on-Trent, have a fine selection of printed tiles and other kinds.

Minton, Hollins & Co., Stoke-on-Trent, make a great variety of mural tiles and others. The subjects for panels covering several tiles—birds by Dixon and W. P. Simpson, also Arthur Simpson; flowers by Buxton; and a mosaic head of Washington—are noticeable.

Craven, Dunnill & Co., Salop, show printed tiles with delicate outlines.

Maw & Co., Broseley, Salop: Among their best patterns are Oriental figures, and tiles in *émail ombrant*. They have executed designs made by Sir Digby Wyatt.

Henry Doulton & Co., Lambeth: The "Lambeth fayence" is now well known—subjects covering many tiles, painted on the biscuit (and glazed afterward) by artists from the Lambeth Art-School—Mr. Bone, Mr. Bennett, Mr. Symonds, Miss Capes, Miss Lewis. The "Departure of the Pilgrims for America in the Seventeenth Century," by Mrs. Sparkes, painted on two hundred and sixty-two tiles, possesses considerable merit. Also, large vases painted with leaves and flowers.

Doulton & Watts, Lambeth: The "Doulton" stone-ware, and the work of the etchers under the glaze—Miss H. Barlow,

Miss Edwards, Mr. James Doulton, Mr. Perky, Mr. Butler—are well known. The beading and artistic embossing are by Mr. G. Tinworth and Mr. A. Barlow.

C. M. CAMPBELL'S process of uniting hexagonal tesseræ of pottery with vitreous cement, in order to produce large surfaces, unwarped and of any form, for ceramic decoration, is of interest. Mr. Moody has designed work executed by Mr. Th. Allen for the South Kensington Museum, by this process. I may also take from my former publication ("Pottery," D. Van Nostrand, publisher, New York) some other names of designers of ceramic decoration in England: R. J. Morris, Walter Lonsdale, W. J. Goode, E. Lessore (deceased), A. Stevens, Coleman, John Gibbs, J. Eyre, J. P. Seddon, Kate Brayford, Lessels, Dr. Dresser, D. Pearce, C. F. Hurten, M. Elden, J. S. Rushton, Ed. Rischgitz, Mrs. D. O. Hill, Aaron Green, C. J. Rowe, A. Waterhouse, T. Morgan, Henry Sherwin, J. Slater, J. H. Wood, J. Randell, J. R. Lees, J. Ellis, Williams and Davis, V. Perling, Miss Mary Tupper, C. Palmere, Steele, D. Lucas, J. Booth, J. Bate, J. Callowhill, J. Hopwich, E. Stephan, W. Cooke, J. S. Whitty, Mitchell, Godfrey Sykes, G. J. Cox, H. Hohle, H. Protat, Pienne, A. Handle.

Among modelers of ceramic statuary and subjects in the round, are: Messrs. Ball, J. Gibson, R. A., F. Fuller, N. Noble, R. A., R. Monti, J. Hadley, W. Theed, L. A. Malempre, T. Wolner, M. C. Belleuse, J. Durham, Westmacott, Papworth, T. Brock, E. M. Miller, P. McDowell, J. Janda, Itzenplitz, Flancock, Wilmore, Mrs. D. O. Hill, Miss S. Terry.

GERMANY.

MERKELBACK & WICK, Grenzhausen, make moderate-priced imitations of mediæval Rhine-ware; also, REIMHOLD HANKE HOHR, near Coblentz.

MAURICE FISCHER, Herend, Hungary, makes reproductions of Sèvres, Dresden, Rococo, Japanese, etc., with considerable success.

JULIUS LETH, at Vienna, makes photos of landscapes, vitrified.

In Berlin, among designers on terra-cotta for E. MARCH, are: C. Fleuse, O. Müller, Prof. Wolff, Blankenstein. On biscuit-ware, are: F. Mantel, Walger.

A. KLAMMERTH, Znaim, Moravia, Austria, makes fayence decorated in the sixteenth-century style.

BRAZIL.

At Rio Janeiro, F. J. ESBERARD and AMARO D. GRILLO make majolica, terra-cotta, and tiles.

RUSSIA.

BONAFEDE, St. Petersburg, makes pieces of a soft terra-cotta body, enameled with opaque colors, somewhat in relief, and with characteristic Russian, Turkish, and Persian patterns, each color being separated by a strong, dark line.

LAVRETSKI, artist and potter, models statues with skill.

SPAIN.

PICKMAN & Co., Seville, for wall-tiles with metallic lustre and Alhambraic patterns; F. G. MONTALBAN, for large, cheap, rudely-painted dishes in Moorish style, and blue figured tiles; M. DE SOTO Y TELLO, for wall-tiles of striking designs; SALVADOR DIEZ, at Manises, for soft earthenware tiles, at one dollar and sixty cents per hundred, may interest the reader.

PORTUGAL.

A. A. DA COSTA, Oporto, for floor-tiles, one to three dollars per hundred; JOAN DE RIO, Oporto, for Della-Robbia statuettes, white, tin-glazed, cheap; M. C. GOMEZ, Mafra, Estremadura, for low-priced ware in Palissy style, may be mentioned.

VARIOUS COUNTRIES. 173

DENMARK.

P. IPSEN'S WIDOW, Copenhagen : Good forms and outlines, and modeling after Thorwaldsen, characterize the work of this manufactory.

ROYAL PORCELAIN-WORKS, Copenhagen : The plaques in relief, after Thorwaldsen, are finely modeled.

SWEDEN.

RORSTRANDS CO., Stockholm, show an admirable fayence chimney-piece, in turquoise, gold, mauve, and lilac, Louis XV. style. Also, good work in ivory-biscuit. Prof. Scholander designs for this firm.

Prof. Molin, Sweden, models ceramic statuary.

ITALY.

We have already had occasion to allude to the names of G. ASCIONE, Naples; BENUCCI E. LATTI, Pesaro, who reproduced the Gubbio lustre ; TAFET TORELLI, Florence, for artistic painting; C. MILLIANI, for good lustres; FARINA ARTISTIC CERAMIC COMPANY, Faenza, for good painting on plaques; TORQUATO CASTELLANI, 80 Via di Poli, Rome, for exact reproductions of sixteenth-century majolica, without the lustre, but in bright colors ; GIUSTINIANI, Naples ; BERTINI, Pisa ; G. BATTA TROJANI, Florence.

BELGIUM.

At Brussels, the work signed Franz Dauge, Adolphe de Mol, Ed. Tourteau, F. X. Volkaërts, Miss Geo. Meunier, and A. Hanstel, is among the best modern fayence-painting. The Belgian school produces charming results ; and, if its treatment of fayence-painting is less well understood than that of the sixteenth century in Italy, it has, at least, avoided the error of treating earthenware like porcelain, and preserved an appropriate freedom of handling.

UNITED STATES.

T. C. SMITH, Union Porcelain-Works, Greenpoint, L. I., New York, makes an excellent quality of hard porcelain, and has successfully established this valuable industry in the United States, with the materials found in the country.

JAMES CARR, 442 West Thirteenth Street, New York, makes stamped designs on terra-cotta under the glaze, a good quality of white-granite and C. C. ware and Parian figures, also fair work in the difficult hard-fire colors; and furthers the progress of ceramic art.

At Trenton, New Jersey, ISAAC DAVIS, COXON & CO., CITY POTTERY COMPANY, JOSEPH H. MOORE, WILLIAM YOUNGS, MERCER POTTERY COMPANY, OTT & BREWER, and Broome, modeler, GREENWOOD POTTERY COMPANY, AMERICAN CROCKERY COMPANY, GLASGOW POTTERY COMPANY, make earthenware of excellent body and glaze, and affording a good basis for decoration.

At Liverpool, Ohio, are LAUGHLIN BROTHERS and the DRESDEN POTTERY COMPANY, in the same line.

At Philadelphia, GALLOWAY & GRAFF make large artistic terra-cotta pieces. Mr. Joseph Wharton shows a deep-blue cobalt color made from the cobalt contained in a nickel-ore from Gap Mine, Lancaster County, Pennsylvania—a valuable possession.

CERAMIC COLORS are obtainable in New York at P. J. Ulrich's, 116 Fourth Avenue, who imports them from Dresden in tubes or powder; also from Mr. George Warrin, 155 West Broadway, who obtains them in powder from England, paints prettily on porcelain, and freely assists those who desire to paint in vitrifiable colors. McCoy & Co., 136 Duane Street, New York; the *Chemisch-technische Fabrik*, Elbogen, Bohemia; A. Lacroix, Rue Parmentier, Paris; E. Greiner Vetters Sohn, Lauscha, near Coburg, Germany, supply colors and lustres.

HOWARD & CO., 222 Fifth Avenue, exhibit charming pieces of modern earthenware from Deck, Worcester Works, Benucci and Latti, A. Klammerth, Copeland, Torelli, etc. Some of the pieces are by the artists, A. Handle, Besch, F. Hurten; and two, with most brilliant enamels, signed by A. Dusson, of Paris, represent—one a plunging dolphin, the other an Eastern scene.

The interest taken in painting on pottery was especially shown in the WOMEN'S PAVILION at the Exhibition. Although this branch of art is a favorite in Europe, it may be regretted that little from that source was represented. Some account of the exhibitors in the United States may be of interest:

Miss M. L. McLaughlin, Cincinnati, showed prettily-painted heads, good in drawing and free in execution; also, Cupids, landscapes, and silhouettes.

Mrs. H. D. Leonard, Cincinnati, carefully-executed storks, flowers, insects, and children's portraits; from the same city were also the Misses L. Keenan, A. Pitman, Rauchfuss, A. Merriam, Eaton, Harrison.

From Paterson, New Jersey, Mrs. Thomas Dale, monochrome subjects, some in bright color. From Newark, New Jersey, Miss S. H. Ward, fairly-drawn tiles, good in treatment, legendary figures, and others; also M. O. Hayes. From Lancaster, Massachusetts, Miss A. H. Whitney and A. C. Chandler, two sets of tiles for chimney-pieces, and grasses and birds, with good effect; also terra-cotta painted in black varnish or oil-paints, and not subsequently fired—a most unsatisfactory process. Mrs. Z. R. Shippen, Jamaica Plains, bright flowers. From Boston, Miss A. H. Cunningham shows good work, vigorous in outline and color; also birds and grasses, freely drawn on tinted grounds, in Japanese style. Miss E. Robbins, berries, ferns, eggs, and leaves, prettily colored. Miss L. M. Marquand, well-drawn subjects, Japanese in character. Miss A. Lee, Japanese figures. Miss E. W. Perkins, a stone-ware jug with expressive modeled head. Miss S. E. Homans, neatly-drawn subjects in brown; Puck, in black on pink; flowers on yellow ground. Miss J. James, Cambridge, cups by seventeen ladies from Lowell, Massachusetts. Among the best work is that of Miss H. S. Mack, Mrs. J. B. Whittaker, Mrs. S. J. Rhodes, Miss

H. A. Whittier, Miss C. Fisk. From New York, Miss A. B. Leggett paints wild grasses; Miss H. E. Ashburner, delicate flowers and grasses; Mrs. W. A. Russell, Roman figures, good in treatment and effect.

The LADIES' ART ASSOCIATION, 896 Broadway, show a variety of work, carefully-painted flowers, etc.

In general, those who have striven after correct outlines, filled in with definite and truthful flat tints—a process which requires some thought and analysis—have also obtained the best results; while too many have wasted valuable time in profusely shading and coloring undefined or somewhat deformed objects, and in working over useless details, as though a part were more important than the whole—an error which has unfortunately characterized at various times many schools at home and abroad. On the whole, the progress made and the interest shown are promising.

CHINA.

The impression prevails that ceramic art is declining in China, though it is difficult to ascertain this. Most of the ware shown is manufactured at King-teh-Chin, and decorated at Shanghai, Kiukiang, and elsewhere. The existence of many old pieces of superior merit does not necessarily prove modern decline, especially when the length of time during which the manufacture has flourished is considered. The Chinese excel in *cloisonné* work on metal, and in harmony of color. Although many objects were exhibited, they were not classified chronologically, so as to facilitate comparisons between the modern and the older wares.

Ho-kan-Chin, Shanghai: collection of old porcelain, some with flowers cut in the paste and filled with glaze, as in Persia.

Kiukiang porcelain is shown by C. F. MOORE, BEAN & JARDINE, etc.

The Imperial Customs of Shanghai show porcelain from Kiangsi; and S. C. ROSE, from King-teh-Chin.

The Imperial Customs of Canton show "Fransee" plates,

for export to France, decorated with figure-subjects in panels on a diapered flowery ground; also plates in the "English Canton" style, distinguished by pink flowers and green leaves on an inharmonious gold ground.

Hukwang Yung, of Hang-chow, shows Kiangsi ware of an unusually brilliant and white body, with Chinese colored figure-subjects.

JAPAN.

Arita, in the province of Hizen, and Tseto, are the porcelain centres. The Hizen porcelain is of a generally hard, vitrescent body; the glaze, somewhat greenish, is also hard and feldspathic, and the decoration is very varied. The blue, sometimes the pink, and lately (at Owari) a green, are used under the glaze. The other colors are applied over the glaze at a subsequent firing. The greenish color of the glaze may be attributed to the lime contained in the ashes (washed to remove the lye), added to the glaze to soften it. Ashes from young and old trees tinge the glaze variously. On the coarser ware the colors are dabbed on rapidly, and often remain in higher relief; while on the finer ware the color is applied carefully, and with a moderate height in the relief. The brownish body of some of the porcelain is dipped in a whiter slip, and upon this a transparent green glaze is laid in the celadon ware. This celadon glaze consists of a stone called *sei-je*, with wood-ashes added. The fine red of the Yeiraku ware is made of oxide of iron; this is applied and fired, and gold is then laid on and scratched into leaf-shapes, fired and burnished. Portions of the gold are dulled by the addition of iron-red, to produce a deadened surface. Some of the minerals used in Japan are: *shina tschi*, plastic clay; *tsuji tschi*, for best thin porcelain, used without other admixture; *ota-kayama*, used as a slip to whiten the body at Arita. *Una tschi* is used for transparent glaze, with addition of wood-ash, cobalt-ore, etc.

The Kaga ware is a porcelain, or a porcelaneous stone-ware (translucent when thin), of a rather porous yellowish body, and not of vitreous fracture; it is sometimes called *Kutani*, "the nine valleys," where the factories of the Prince of Kaga are situated; it is usually decorated elaborately in red and gold, with occasional blue and green marks. At Owari, large, and at Mino, small ware, of fine porcelain in blue and gold, is made, often decorated at Tokio.

The Banko ware is a stone-ware approaching porcelain, usually brown, sometimes white body, and unglazed. One variety, however, is glazed in black, and decorated in colors.

Satsuma, Awata, and Kiyoto pottery is of a cream-colored body, and crackled. The Satsuma is paler, of coarser fracture, and decorated in gold with a little color. The Japanese sometimes point with pride to the deep color of the stains of their old crackled teacups, showing their long use in the family. The practical inconvenience of a *crazed glaze*, namely, that the body absorbs liquids through the cracks (which, if organic, are slowly decomposed), limits its use to decorative pieces, boxes, etc., in Japan, as it should with us. The Awata is of fine quality, hard almost as stone-ware, decorated in enamel colors, and sometimes gold. At Kiyoto, also at Shibei, in Tokei, and at Awaji, Awata ware is also made.

The *cloisonné* work on Awata earthenware has taken considerable development since 1873, and is conducted as follows: A glazed piece is taken, the glaze scraped away with sandstone, and a flat brass wire is attached temporarily in the requisite shape, with orchis-root glue. A fusible lead glass is added as a cement. The cloisons are filled with enamel mixed with water, and the piece is fired. The enamel usually contracts; the interstices are filled and fired again several times; the piece is finally rubbed and polished.

The Japanese also apply *cloisonné* work on porcelain, and vary the effect by using various breadths of wire and silver wire. The labor of *cloisonné* work is greater than that of painting, but it produces effects by a depth of enamels which in painting would fuse together. Also the varied play of light on the metallic threads is richer than a mere flat gold or silver outline.

S. Fukaomi, of the porcelain-factory of Koransha, at Arita, province of Hizen—a large manufacturer—uses colors of great brilliancy, applied with taste. Signs his name "Kisa." (*See* mark.)

K. Tsuji, of Koransha, shows pierced work—a beautiful pink; also, pieces with handles cast in a plaster-of-Paris mould, a process learned by the Japanese at Vienna in 1870. (*See* mark.)

Ckaki Shosha, Kiyoto, exhibited a collection of old porcelain, showing the beginning of Kioto porcelain two hundred years old; in dark monochrome.

Kirio-Kosho-Kuwaisha: a collection of old porcelain, and some pottery one thousand years old, and some old Satsuma.

Ch. Minoda, Tokio, also an old collection.

Wage Kitei, Kioto: pottery and porcelain; some ornaments are embossed or in relief; curious movable handles; good examples of Awata ware.

Takashi Dohachi, Kioto: porcelain and earthenware; the first decorated in imitation of the European; bluish glaze. Shows also a vase colored red and decorated by reserving spaces in the white ground—a process learned by the Japanese at Vienna in 1870. The Dohachi family have made porcelain for two hundred and thirty years.

Kanzan Denshishi, Kiomidzu, in Kioto, decorates porcelain in imitation of inlaid bronze, in a style called "Zogan," originated by himself. Also copies of red Yeiraku ware. (*See* mark.)

Y. Fukagawa makes large pieces of porcelain, beautifully decorated; notably a pair of vases eight feet high, potted in two pieces, one portion being six feet high in one piece, decorated in blue on white ground with red, gold, and lacquer in low-relief, with chimerical and grotesque subjects; vases five feet six inches, fired in muffle-furnaces made on purpose for them; circular dishes, three feet diameter, beautifully decorated with flowers, fish, pheasants, etc.; also large plateaux. Make their own colors. (*See* mark.)

Seifu Yohei, Kiyoto: vases of white porcelain, with

slipped and vermiculated ornament, highly glazed; also vases with white reserves on red.

MASHIMIDZU ZOROKU, Kiyoto, makes porcelain decorated in blue under the glaze—a style very popular with the Japanese, and characteristic. That of Kiyoto is well known. Also celadon ware.

SHIMIDZU KAMESHICHI, Kiyoto, makes similar celadon ware; shows a service in white porcelain, of fruit-shaped pieces decorated with small colored figures.

ZENGARO YEIRAKU, Kiyoto, makes the ware with red ground and gold decoration, called Yeiraku ware, a specialty of the family. The ornament is branched and continuous, like the Hindoo. Some of the red is of unusual brilliancy for porcelain; this color came from China, but Yeiraku used it skillfully. Imitations of inlaid bronze, in porcelain; also beautiful celadon glazed pieces, and vases with a ground of powdered gold surrounding irregular panels, decorated each with separate subjects. (*See* mark.)

KATO GOSUKE, Tajimimura, province of Mino: small pieces. Porcelain, sometimes warped, decorated in blue under the glaze; figures outlined in gold, and birds colored in faint gray; flowers in European style, not so good as the Japanese.

MAKUDZU KOZAN, Yokohama: porcelain vases with relief figures, such as crabs with movable eyes, curiously and well executed; fine *pâte-sur-pâte*, modeling and splashed colors cleverly combined in a vase representing the gods of Wind and Thunder; pedestal, curiously wrought like coral-work; also earthenware, which began in imitation of Satsuma, and added figures in relief, and intricate perforated work. Moderate prices. (*See* mark.)

G. WATEYA, Kanazawa, Kaga Province, makes Kaga ware —a hard porcelaneous stone-ware, coarse creamy or ivory body, strong colors and gilding.

Y. YOSHIDA, Kanazawa, Kaga: large bowls, decorated, of porcelaneous stone-ware.

P. AWO, Kanazawa, Kaga: flower-pots, ivory body, red and gold.

T. HEKIZAN, Kanazawa, Kaga : Kaga style ; large pieces ; gold outline.

S. SEIKAN, Kanazawa : Kaga ware painted with great delicacy ; glaze defective.

T. SHOZA, Kanazawa : an old-established manufactory, that maintains the vigorous style of early Kaga ware ; same defects of glaze.

A. SETZUZAN, Kanazawa : Kaga ware of fair quality.

S. HARUNA, Kanazawa : Kaga ware ; well-drawn decoration, notably a snow-storm, and sea-side scenes.

MUNEAKI, Kanazawa : Kaga ware ; fair quality ; vermiculated gold on red.

K. UTSUMI, Kanazawa : Kaga ware ; fine vases, representing a priest entering a temple ; a vase with ten fish, subjects in panels, on the ordinary red and gold Kaga ground ; a vase with three-clawed dragon, and dark clouds worked over with gold and silver lines.

CHIUJI, Kanazawa : delicately-executed forms, and decoration in the early Kaga style ; dragon-shaped handle.

K. SHINODA, province of Kaga, introduced delicate painting on panels ; good drawing, profuse gilding ; notable for precision of workmanship. (*See* mark.)

HIYOCHIYEN, Tokio : porcelain made at Arita, Owari, and elsewhere, is decorated at Tokio by Hiyochiyen, who marks his name in red on the ware, while the blue mark is that of the porcelain. Some designs are by Notomi. The designs of Itchiraku and Shinzan are praised by Mr. Notomi as the best. The drawing is neat, and very delicate. Subjects : comic tortoise ; quails with white enamel-drops in relief ; vase with octopus and crawfish in relief, designed by Notomi ; vase with fish and enamel-drops in the sea ; fan-shaped plaques, with delicate painting and a very fine red color. (*See* mark.)

M. NAKAYAMA, Kuwana, Ise : modern banko or demi-porcelain ; a dish with crayfish and crabs, cleverly executed : decoration medium.

JEWBEI IIDA, Nagoya, province of Owari, shows many fine

pieces of porcelain from the three following makers: Gosuke, flower-pots, tea-services in the old style of dark blue under the glaze, and occasional chrome-green, moderate in price; Hanske, tea-sets and plaques painted in a paler blue, with varied subjects; Kawamoto, large plaques, generally with bold leaves, etc., left in white on a deep-blue ground; occasional gilding, and panels in blue and white; "Kiko," or turtle-back ornament; a new bronze color of some lustre.

S. Fukihara, Tokio: *cloisonné* enamel on porcelain.

Shippo Kuwaisha, Nagoya, Owari: *cloisonné* on porcelain, of rich effect and harmonious combinations. (*See* mark.)

Tanzan Seikai, Kiyoto, shows an experimental photograph on earthenware; maker of Awata ware, who also makes porcelain; colors somewhat dull; sometimes copies European decoration.

Kinkozan-Sobei, Kiyoto: cheap Awata ware; fairly made; teapots, bamboo-shaped, modeled by hand.

Shimidzu Rokubei, Kiyoto: East-Indian wine-pot form for "saki" wine; some imitation of European styles; colors impure. Also "*Topa ye*," or painting in the style of Topa, a priest who is said to have lived six hundred years ago in Topa, and painted in a grotesque, somewhat coarse style, in red outline with additions in gold.

Shimidzu Kameshichi, Kiyoto: Awata ware, made in tea and coffee sets for European purchasers. The Japanese do not themselves use this crackled ware for tea, excepting occasionally the Satsuma.

Ch. Tsuji, Kiyoto: Awata toilet-services, with delicately-painted subjects from Nature, in the genuine Japanese manner.

Taizan Yohei, Kiyoto: Awata ware of a fine body, in special shapes for Europeans; also handsome *cloisonné* work on earthenware.

Kashiu Shampei, Ingano Mura, province of Awaji, makes Awaji ware resembling the Awata, but of finer body and harder glaze; excellent decoration; also a hard stone-ware, almost porcelaneous.

SHITOMEI SOHEI, Yokka-ichi, province of Ise, makes Banko ware, so called after the inventor; also inlaid stone-ware of a white body inlaid clear through a red body, showing inside and outside; moulded by hand; also a body resembling that of Wedgwood, sometimes coated with a white slip inside, celebrated in Japan for its solidity and lightness; also teapots of a marbled body, called *Nokume*, or "veined."

Y. MORI, Yakka-ichi, Ise: Banko ware; also earthenware, soft, green glazed.

NAKASHIMA, Kagoshima, province of Satsuma: very large vases, of body shaped like wicker-work and somewhat dull colors.

BENSHI, Kiyoto: small terra-cotta figures of great expression. Legendary subjects: The devil, disguised as a grandmother, regaining his lost arm; Chinji Hachelo, a hero of great strength, finds three men strong enough together to bend his bow; a wicked old woman essaying to kill a young girl, who is protected by her prayers to her deity.

REFERENCES.

IN studying ornament, it will be observed that the *Persian* ranks foremost in Oriental ornament, since it combines purity of line with harmonious balance and distribution of form and color. The *Hindoo*, inferior in line, is also admirable in distribution and color. The *Chinese*, also inferior in line, is equally admirable in harmony of color; while the *Raffaelesque*, of which good examples are rare, is nevertheless the style of greatest promise, since it is spiritual in expression and ideal in conception, and introduces superior drawing and greater variety in the tones of colors. It is also correspondingly difficult to succeed in, and rarely equals the Oriental in distribution of form or harmony of color.

Excellent remarks on composition, applicable to ornament, are found in Da Vinci's "Treatise," De Lairesse, Flaxman, C. Blanc, Taine, F. Moody's "Lectures;" on balance of form and color, in the works of Owen Jones, Racinet, Dresser, Redgrave; on Persian ornament, in Flandin and Coste, Chardin, Jacquemart, Racinet; on pottery-marks, in Chaffers, T. Graesse, Castellani Catalogue; on technical manufacture, in A. Brongniart, C. Piccolpasso, D. Magnier; on the history and illustrations of majolica, in G. Passeri, Lazari, Campori, Fortnum, Darcel, Delange, Piot, Jacquemart, Marryatt, and A. Castellani.

DECORATIVE DESIGN. 185

In Fig. 51 I have endeavored to apply some of the propositions alluded to in these pages, in a design for a decorative piece, or votive disk.

FIG. 51.

THE END.

A SUPERB NEW WORK BY LACROIX.

THE EIGHTEENTH CENTURY.

THE MANNERS, CUSTOMS, AND COSTUMES OF THE EIGHTEENTH CENTURY, IN FRANCE, 1700-1789.

Illustrated with twenty-one magnificent Chromo-lithographs (art-gems in themselves), and *three hundred and fifty* highly-finished Wood-Engravings after Watteau, Vanloo, Rigaud, Boucher, Lancret, J. Vernet, Chardin, Jeaurat, Beauchardon, Saint-Aubin, Eisen, Gravelot, Moreau, Cochin, Wille, Debucourt, etc. The designs, lithographs, and engravings, all executed by eminent artists, under the direction of M. Racinet, the well-known author of "Polychromatic Ornament." In one sumptuous volume, imperial 8vo, cloth, emblematic gilt sides, and gilt edges, $15; half calf, $18; calf, $21; tree calf, $28; morocco, extra, $24.

The comprehensive character of this work will be appreciated more fully by noting contents, embracing, as they do, the social ranks and customs, the public occupations, amusements, etc., of "La Belle France," as follows, viz.:

1. The King and the Court.
2. The Nobles.
3. The Bourgeoisie.
4. The People.
5. The Army and Navy.
6. The Clergy.
7. The Parliament.
8. The Finances.
9. Commerce.
10. Education.
11. Charities.
12. Justice and Police.
13. Aspect of Paris.
14. Fêtes and Pleasures of Paris.
15. The Cuisine and Table.
16. The Theatres.
17. The Salons.
18. Voyages, etc.
19. Costumes and Modes.

*** The splendid success of the various works of M. Lacroix, on the "Manners, Customs, and Dress, during the Middle Ages, and during the Renaissance," suggested the preparation of a work of a similar character, on the "Institutions, Manners, and Dress, in France, during the Eighteenth Century." This sumptuous volume is a brilliant exhibition of every grade of life and society in France, from 1700 to 1789. The work is illustrated with 21 full-page Chromo-lithographs, richly colored, and 350 beautiful Engravings on Wood. These illustrations are copied with the utmost care from the original paintings of the best and most esteemed artists of the eighteenth century, and in beauty of design, exquisite finish, and the real interest of their subjects, far surpass any similar productions. The typographical excellence, and elaborate and appropriate binding, combined with its intrinsic literary and artistic value, render it one of the richest volumes ever published.

OTHER WORKS BY THE SAME AUTHOR.

THE ARTS IN THE MIDDLE AGES, and at the Period of the Renaissance. By PAUL LACROIX, Curator of the Imperial Library of the Arsenal, Paris. Illustrated with 19 Chromo-lithographic Prints by Kellerhoven, and upward of 400 Engravings on Wood. 1 vol., imperial 8vo, cloth, gilt sides and back. 520 pages. Price, $12; half calf, $15; half morocco, $15; full calf, $18; full morocco, $25.

MANNERS, CUSTOMS, AND DRESS, DURING THE MIDDLE AGES, and during the Renaissance Period. By PAUL LACROIX. Illustrated with 15 Chromo-lithographic Prints by F. Kellerhoven, and upward of 400 Engravings on Wood. 1 vol., royal 8vo. Half morocco, price, $12; half morocco, extra, $15; half calf, $15; calf, $18; tree calf, $25; morocco, extra, $21; morocco, super extra, $25.

MILITARY AND RELIGIOUS LIFE IN THE MIDDLE AGES, and at the Period of the Renaissance. By PAUL LACROIX. Illustrated with 14 Chromo-lithographic Prints by J. Kellerhoven, Réjamey, and L. Allard, and upward of 400 Engravings on Wood. 1 vol., royal 8vo. Half bound, $12; half calf and morocco, $15; calf, $18; tree calf, $25; morocco, extra, $21; super extra, $25.

D. APPLETON & CO., PUBLISHERS,

549 & 551 *Broadway, New York.*

BRYANT'S POETICAL WORKS.

A NEW ILLUSTRATED EDITION.

1 vol., small 4to. With 100 Illustrations by Birket Foster, Harry Fenn, Alfred Fredericks, and others.

Price, in cloth, gilt edges, $4; morocco, extra, $8; tree calf, $10.

From the Tribune.

"This new and beautiful edition should have a permanent place in every intelligent household in the country. The paper, typography, and illustrations, are alike excellent, and fitly embalm the life's work of one of the chief founders of our literature."

From the Philadelphia Inquirer.

"It is not too much to say that, in the United States, Bryant stands in the first rank, to which he was admitted quite early in his literary life, when the decided evidence of brilliancy he had given in 'Thanatopsis' had been more than sustained."

From the Hartford Post.

"In every respect the work is an excellent contribution to the publications of the year, and Mr. Bryant may well congratulate himself on the superb setting which his jewels of thought have been favored with."

From the Northern Christian Advocate.

"What new thing can be said of our laureate? He who has enriched our literature with beauty after beauty during threescore years, whom our Legislature has stooped to reverence, and to whom the people have presented such a tribute of esteem as was never offered to any writer on this continent before, and yet whose writings always came forth spontaneously, unpurchased, needs not to be advertised now."

From the Albany Times.

"His name is classical in the literature of the language. Wherever English poetry is read and loved, his poems are known by heart. Others before him have sung the beauties of creation and the greatness of God, but no one ever observed external things more closely, or transferred his impressions to paper in more vivid colors."

From the Boston Journal.

"The book is one well worthy of the poet's honored age, and will be welcomed by his many admirers. Beautifully printed, illustrated with 100 engravings from drawings by Birket Foster, Harry Fenn, Alfred Fredericks, and others, and very tastefully bound. It embraces all of Mr. Bryant's poetical works, down to and including 'The Flood of Years,' the poem which attracted this year such marked attention."

New York: D. APPLETON & CO., Publishers, 549 & 551 Broadway.

THE LIFE OF
HIS ROYAL HIGHNESS
THE PRINCE CONSORT.
By THEODORE MARTIN.

With Portraits and Views. Vols. I. & II. now ready. 12mo. Cloth. Per vol., $2.

"The book, indeed, is more comprehensive than its title implies. Purporting to tell the life of the Prince Consort, it includes a scarcely less minute biography—which may be regarded as almost an autobiography—of the Queen herself; and, when it is complete, it will probably present a more minute history of the domestic life of a queen and her 'master' (the term is Her Majesty's) than has ever before appeared."—*From the Athenæum.*

"Mr. Martin has accomplished his task with a success which could scarcely have been anticipated. His biography of Prince Albert would be valuable and instructive even if it were addressed to remote and indifferent readers who had no special interest in the English court or in the royal family. Prince Albert's actual celebrity is inseparably associated with the high position which he occupied, but his claim to permanent reputation depends on the moral and intellectual qualities which were singularly adapted to the circumstances of his career. In any rank of life he would probably have attained distinction; but his prudence, his self-denial, and his aptitude for acquiring practical knowledge, could scarcely have found a more suitable field of exercise than in his peculiar situation as the acknowledged head of a constitutional monarchy."—*From the Saturday Review.*

"The author writes with dignity and grace, he values his subject, and treats him with a certain courtly reverence, yet never once sinks into the panegyrist, and while apparently most frank—so frank, that the reticent English people may feel the intimacy of his domestic narratives almost painful—he is never once betrayed into a momentary indiscretion. The almost idyllic beauty of the relation between the Prince Consort and the Queen comes out as fully as in all previous histories of that relation—and we have now had three—as does also a good deal of evidence as to the Queen's own character, hitherto always kept down, and, as it were, self-effaced in publications written or sanctioned by herself."—*From the London Spectator.*

"Of the abilities which have been claimed for the Prince Consort, this work affords us small means of judging. But of his wisdom, strong sense of duty, and great dignity and purity of character, the volume furnishes ample evidence. In this way it will be of service to any one who reads it."—*From the New York Evening Post.*

"There is a striking contrast between this volume and the Greville Memoirs, which relate to a period in English history immediately preceding Prince Albert's marriage with Queen Victoria. Radical changes were effected in court-life by Victoria's accession to the throne. . . . In the work before us, which is the unfolding of a model home-life, a life in fact unrivaled in the abodes of modern royalty, there is nothing but what the purest mind can read with real pleasure and profit.

"Mr. Martin draws a most exquisite portraiture of the married life of the royal pair, which seems to have been as nearly perfect as any thing human can be. The volume closes shortly after the Revolution of 1848, at Paris, when Louis Philippe and his hapless queen were fleeing to England in search of an asylum from the fearful forebodings which overhung their pathway. It was a trying time for England, but, says Mr. Martin with true dramatic effect in the closing passages of his book: 'When the storm burst, it found him prepared. In rising to meet the difficulties of the hour, the prince found the best support in the cheerful courage of the queen,' who on the 4th of April of that same year wrote to King Leopold: 'I never was calmer and quieter or less nervous. Great events make me calm; it is only trifles that irritate my nerves.' Thus ends the first volume of one of the most important biographies of the present time. The second volume will follow as soon as its preparation can be effected."—*From the Hartford Evening Post.*

D. APPLETON & CO., Publishers, 549 & 551 Broadway, N. Y.

THE GREVILLE MEMOIRS.

COMPLETE IN TWO VOLS.

A JOURNAL OF THE REIGNS OF
King George IV. & King William IV.

By the Late CHAS. C. F. GREVILLE, Esq.,

Clerk of the Council to those Sovereigns.

Edited by HENRY REEVE, Registrar of the Privy Council.

12mo. PRICE, $4.00.

This edition contains the complete text as published in the three volumes of the English edition.

"The sensation created by these Memoirs, on their first appearance, was not out of proportion to their real interest. They relate to a period of our history second only in importance to the Revolution of 1688; they portray manners which have now disappeared from society, yet have disappeared so recently that middle-aged men can recollect them; and they concern the conduct of very eminent persons, of whom some are still living, while of others the memory is so fresh that they still seem almost to be contemporaneous."—*The Academy.*

"Such Memoirs as these are the most interesting contributions to history that can be made, and the most valuable as well. The man deserves gratitude from his posterity who, being placed in the midst of events that have any importance, and of people who bear any considerable part in them, sits down day by day and makes a record of his observations."—*Buffalo Courier.*

"The Greville Memoirs, already in a third edition in London, in little more than two months, have been republished by D. Appleton & Co., New York. The three loosely-printed English volumes are here given in two, without the slightest abridgment, and the price, which is nine dollars across the water, here is only four. It is not too much to say that this work, though not so ambitious in its style as Horace Walpole's well-known 'Correspondence,' is much more interesting. In a word, these Greville Memoirs supply valuable materials not alone for political, but also for social history during the time they cover. They are additionally attractive from the large quantity of racy anecdotes which they contain."—*Philadelphia Press.*

"These are a few among many illustrations of the pleasant, gossipy information conveyed in these Memoirs, whose great charm is the free and straightforward manner in which the writer chronicles his impressions of men and events."—*Boston Daily Globe.*

"As will be seen, these volumes are of remarkable interest, and fully justify the encomiums that heralded their appearance in this country. They will attract a large circle of readers here, who will find in their gossipy pages an almost inexhaustible fund of instruction and amusement."—*Boston Saturday Evening Gazette.*

"Since the publication of Horace Walpole's Letters, no book of greater historical interest has seen the light than the Greville Memoirs. It throws a curious, and, we may almost say, a terrible light on the conduct and character of the public men in England under the reigns of George IV. and William IV. Its descriptions of those kings and their kinsfolk are never likely to be forgotten."—*N. Y. Times.*

D. APPLETON & CO., PUBLISHERS, 549 & 551 Broadway, N. Y.

UNIFORM WITH "GERMAN HOME LIFE."

FRENCH HOME LIFE.

Reprinted from Blackwood.

1 VOL., 12MO. CLOTH. PRICE, $1.50.

OPINIONS OF THE PRESS.

New York Tribune.

"The way in which their neighbors live is always an object of curiosity with a large class of inquiring minds that can find no other vent for the divine energies of their nature. It is not often that the subject falls into the hands of persons with so much good sense and just perceptive powers, as the author of this volume. He professes to have resided in France for many years, and, in fact, to have found a second home in that country, so that he is entitled to speak with the freedom and authority of personal experience. At all events, he shows an equal familiarity with the domestic customs of England and of France, his comparisons are often piquant as well as informing, and if he lifts the roof from many a private *ménage* in the capital, it is because he can disclose nothing to disadvantage in the interior."

Boston Journal.

"The Appletons publish an interesting volume on 'French Home Life,' reprinted from *Blackwood's Magazine*. The author has lived among the French for twenty-five years or more, and has made a study of their character and ways of life. The book is fresh and entertaining in style, and conveys a good deal of information."

Episcopal Register.

"The writer of this volume, an Englishman, has lived for a quarter of a century in France, amid ties and affections which have made that country his second home. He tells us, pleasantly and instructively, of French children, food, manners, language, furniture, dress, marriage, and servants, conveying much authentic information upon these interesting topics. The fact that this series of papers originally appeared in *Blackwood's Magazine* proves their high character."

The Presbyterian.

"The book is one of decided interest, full of every-day affairs, of home life, the life which is passed under a roof and at a fireside. The themes are Servants, Children, Furniture, Food, Manners, Dress, etc. The style is very pleasant, and the book one which throws much light on the real state of French society."

D. APPLETON & CO., PUBLISHERS,
549 & 551 *Broadway, New York.*

RECENT PUBLICATIONS.

Diseases of Modern Life. By Dr. B. W. RICHARDSON, F. R. S. 1 vol., 12mo. Cloth. $2.00.

"'Diseases of Modern Life' is a work which throws so much light on what it is of the utmost importance for the public to know, that it deserves to be thoroughly and generally read."—*Graphic.*

"The literature on preventive medicine has received no more valuable contribution than this admirably-written treatise by one of the most accomplished physicians of Great Britain, who has concentrated upon his task a great amount of scientific research and clinical experience. No book that we have ever read more fully merits the attention of the intelligent public, to whom it is addressed."—*The World.*

Comin' Thro' the Rye. 1 vol., 8vo. Paper covers. 75 cents.

"A very amusing and well-written story. The history of the youth of the Adairs is extremely amusing, and told in a bright and witty manner. . . . One of the pleasantest novels of the season."—*Morning Post.*

"It is a clever novel, never dull, and the story never hangs fire."—*Standard.*

Memoir and Correspondence of Caroline Herschel. By Mrs. JOHN HERSCHEL. With Portraits. 12mo. Cloth. $1.75.

"The unlimited admiration excited by the noble, heroic virtues, and the uncommon talents of the subject of the memoir, is overborne by the intense sympathy felt for her long life of unselfish and unregretted devotion to others."—*Chicago Tribune.*

General History of Greece, from the Earliest Period to the Death of Alexander the Great. By the Rev. GEORGE W. COX. 1 vol., 12mo. Cloth. $2.50.

"We envy those schoolboys and undergraduates who will make their first acquaintance with Greek history through Mr. Cox's admirable volume. It ought to supersede all the popular Histories of Greece which have gone before it."—*The Hour.*

"The book is worthy, in every way, of the author's reputation. . . . It is altogether a most interesting and valuable book."—*Educational Times.*

A Short History of Natural Science and of the Progress of Discovery from the Time of the Greeks to the Present Day. By ARABELLA B. BUCKLEY. With Illustrations. 1 vol., 12mo. $2.00.

"Miss Buckley, the friend of Sir Charles Lyell, and for many years the secretary of the great geologist, in this volume has given a continuous, methodical, and complete sketch of the main discoveries of science from the time of Thales, one of the seven wise men, B. C. 700, down to the present day. The work is unique in its way, being the first attempt ever made to produce a brief and simple history of science. The author has entirely succeeded in her labors, evincing judgment, learning, and literary skill."—*Episcopal Register.*

A Hand-Book of Architectural Styles. Translated from the German by W. COTLETT-SANDERS. 1 vol., 8vo. With 639 Illustrations. $6.00.

"There is a great amount of information in the book, in a small compass. For one who simply wishes to gain a full knowledge of the various styles of architecture, written in a clear and interesting manner, the volume has not its equal nor rival in the English language. This knowledge will be facilitated by the profuse illustrations, of which there are not less than six hundred and thirty-nine, nearly all handsome specimens of engraving, among which figure a large number of famous buildings, ancient and modern."—*Evening Mail.*

D. APPLETON & CO., 549 & 551 Broadway, N. Y.

www.ingramcontent.com/pod-product-compliance
Lightning Source LLC
Chambersburg PA
CBHW030820190426
43197CB00036B/676